JN025077

# What If?

Serious
Scientific Answers
to Absurd Hypothetical
Questions

*Edited by Aki Kobayashi*

SHOHAKUSHA

# FOREWORD

　本テキストは、ランドール・マンロー(Randall Munroe, 1984- ) の *What If?: Serious Scientific Answers To Absurd Hypothetical Questions* (2014) から 15 のトピックを抜粋し、語学教材として編集したものです。

　「野球のボールを光速で投げたらどうなるか？」、「すべての人間が一か所に集まってジャンプしたらどうなるか？」、「モグラ(mole)を一か所に 1 モル(mole)集めたらどうなるか？」といった突拍子もない質問に、著者が科学・数学の知識とマンガを使ってユーモラスに答える原著は、2014 年に出版されるやいなや、たちまちベストセラーになりました。著者のランドール・マンローは、クリストファー・ニューポート大学で物理学を学んだ後、NASA のラングレー研究所でロボット開発に従事し、その後ウェブコミック作家へと転身した異色の経歴を持つ人物です。原著は、マンローが運営するウェブサイト 'wkcd' (https://xkcd.com/1652/) から派生した読者投稿サイト 'What If'のウェブコミックがもとになっています。本テキストの内容が気に入った方は、是非こちらも覗いてみてください。

　本文の後には、

　(1) Comprehension Check

　(2) Writing a Summary

　(3) Discussion

を付しています。(1) は、本文の内容が理解できているかを確認する正誤問題 (True or False) と、文中の語彙の意味を確認する問題を TOEFL® のフォーマットで解くことによって読解力を高めることを目的にしています。(2) は、本文中に登場する専門用語の意味を平易な英語で説明する問題と、100 words 程度で内容を要約する問題を用意しました。専門用語を説明する際には、文中の語彙を利用しつつも、辞書やインターネットを積極的に活用することをお勧めします。(3) は、題材について発展的な学習を促すためのものです。

　*What if ?* で英語を学んだらどうなるだろうか？

　本テキストが英語と科学双方への関心を高める一助になることを願っています。

　最後になりますが、本テキストの作成には松柏社の森有紀子氏に大変お世話になりました。本書は森氏からの呼びかけがあって生まれたものです。記して御礼申し上げます。

　2019 年秋　　　　　　　　　　　　　　　　　　　　　　　　　編著者

---

▶ Reading 本文中の語句の右肩に付いている番号は、99 頁〜の Randall Munroe による原注番号を示しています。

# CONTENTS

# UNIT 1
# RELATIVISTIC
# BASEBALL
相対論的野球

 **Prepare to discuss and share your opinion**

光速 90 パーセントの剛速球で投げた野球のボールを打ち返したら、どんなことが起こるだろうか。

## ◁ABC **Vocabulary**

Look up the following words and phrases in a dictionary.

| | | | | |
|---|---|---|---|---|
| stationary | vibrate | jostle | fuse | trigger |
| collision | ram | disintegrate | shred | be eligible to |

## What would happen if you tried to hit a baseball pitched at 90 percent the speed of light?

—Ellen McManis

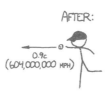

*Let's set aside the question of how we got the baseball moving that fast. We'll suppose it's a normal pitch, except in the instant the pitcher releases the ball, it magically accelerates to 0.9c. From that point onward, everything proceeds according to normal physics.* ✎ **0.9c** 'c' は光速度

🍎

4

ANSWER

 **Reading** ━━━━━━━━━━━━━━━━━━━━━━━━━━━━━━━━ 🔊 Audio 1-02

**1** THE ANSWER TURNS OUT to be "a lot of things," and they all happen very quickly, and it doesn't end well for the batter (or the pitcher). I sat down with some physics books, a Nolan Ryan action figure, and a bunch of videotapes of nuclear tests and tried to sort it all out. What follows is my best guess at a nanosecond-by-nanosecond portrait. ₅

**2** The ball would be going so fast that everything else would be practically stationary. Even the molecules in the air would stand still. Air molecules would vibrate back and forth at a few hundred miles per hour, but the ball would be moving through them at 600 million miles per hour. This means that as far as the ball is concerned, they would just be hanging there, frozen. ₁₀

**3** The ideas of aerodynamics wouldn't apply here. Normally, air would flow around anything moving through it. But the air molecules in front of this ball wouldn't have time to be jostled out of the way. The ball would smack into them so hard that the atoms in the air molecules would actually fuse with the atoms in the ball's surface. Each collision would release a burst ₁₅ gamma rays and scattered particles.[1]

  **4** These gamma rays and debris would expand outward in a bubble centered on the pitcher's mound. They would ₂₀ start to tear apart the molecules in the air, ripping the electrons from the nuclei and turning the air in the stadium into an expanding bubble of incandescent plasma. The wall of this bubble would approach the batter at about the speed of light — only slightly ahead of the ball itself.

**5** The constant fusion at the front of the ball would push back on it, slowing ₂₅ it down, as if the ball were a rocket flying tail-first while firing its engines. Unfortunately, the ball would be going so fast that even the tremendous force from this ongoing thermonuclear explosion would barely slow it down at all. It would, however, start to eat away at the surface, blasting tiny fragments of the ball in all directions. These fragments would be going so fast that when ₃₀ they hit air molecules, they would trigger two or three more rounds of fusion.

**6** After about 70 nanoseconds the ball would arrive at home plate. The batter wouldn't even have seen the pitcher let go of the ball, since the light carrying that information would arrive at about the same time the ball would. Collisions with the air would have eaten the ball away almost ₃₅ completely, and it would now be a bullet-shaped cloud of expanding plasma (mainly carbon, oxygen, hydrogen, and nitrogen) ramming into the air and triggering more fusion as it went. The shell of x-rays would hit the batter first, and a handful of nanoseconds later the debris cloud would hit.

40 **7** When it would reach home plate, the center of the cloud would still be moving at an appreciable fraction of the speed of light. It would hit the
45 bat first, but then the batter, plate, and catcher would all be scooped up and carried backward through the backstop as they disintegrated. The shell of x-rays and superheated plasma would expand outward and upward, swallowing the backstop, both teams, the stands, and the surrounding neighborhood — all in the first microsecond.

50 **8** Suppose you're watching from a hilltop outside the city. The first thing you would see would be a blinding light, far outshining the sun. This would gradually fade over the course of a few seconds, and a growing fireball would rise into a mushroom cloud. Then, with a great roar, the blast wave would arrive, tearing up trees and shredding houses.

55 **9** Everything within roughly a mile of the park would be leveled, and a firestorm would engulf the surrounding city. The baseball diamond, now a sizable crater, would be centered a few hundred feet behind the former location of the backstop.

**10** Major League Baseball Rule
60 6.08(b) suggests that in this situation, the batter would be considered "hit by pitch," and would be eligible to advance to first base.

---

**Notes**

**1** **Nolan Ryan** ノーラン・ライアン。アメリカのプロ野球選手。大リーグ史上、シーズン最多奪三振記録・通算最多奪三振記録保持者。"The Express" の異名を持つ。
**nanosecond-by-nanosecond** 1ナノ秒ごと
**2** **air molecule** 空気分子
**3** **aerodynamics** 空気力学　**gamma rays** ガンマ線
**4** **debris** （核融合生成物の）破片　**electron** 電子　**plasma** プラズマ
**5** **fusion** 核融合　**thermonuclear** 原子核融合反応の
**6** **bullet shaped** 弾丸形の　**carbon, oxygen, hydrogen, and nitrogen** 炭素、酸素、水素、窒素
**10** **Major League Baseball Rule** メジャーリーグ・ベースボール規則　**hit by pitch** 死球

## Comprehension Check

 **A** Read the sentences below and choose T(true) or F(false).

1. The ball would be going so fast that everything else would be active. **T / F**

2. The ball would smash into them so hard that the atoms in the air molecules would actually merge with the atoms in the ball's surface. **T / F**

3. These x-rays and debris would expand outward in a bubble centered on the pitcher's mound. **T / F**

4. The batter would not even have seen the pitcher let go of the ball, because the light carrying that information would arrive at about the same time the ball would. **T / F**

5. Major League Baseball Rule 6.08(b) indicates that in this situation, the batter would be considered "hit by pitch," and would have the right to proceed to first base. **T / F**

**B** Select the best answer for each question.

1. In Paragraph 1-6, the author claims that
   (A) the ball would be going so fast that everything else would not be practically stationary.
   (B) these x-rays and debris would start to tear apart the molecules in the air, ripping the electrons from the nuclei and turning the air in the stadium into an expanding bubble of incandescent plasma.
   (C) tiny fragments of the ball would be going so fast that when they hit air molecules, they would trigger two or three more rounds of fusion.
   (D) the shell of gamma rays would hit the catcher first, and a handful of nanoseconds later the debris cloud would hit.

2. The word "trigger" in Paragraph 5 is closest in meaning to
   (A) destroy
   (B) set off
   (C) prevent
   (D) block

3. The word "collisions" in Paragraph 6 is closest in meaning to
   (A) construction
   (B) compliment
   (C) creation
   (D) crash

4. The word "disintegrate" in Paragraph 7 is closest in meaning to
   (A) combine
   (B) put together
   (C) break down
   (D) develop

 **Writing a Summary**

**A** Determine the main idea of the following keywords.

1. fusion

2. gamma rays

3. plasma

4. hit by pitch

**B** Summarize the passage in about 100 words.

_____

_____

_____

_____

_____

_____

**Discussion**

Discuss and share your opinion on "Relativistic Football".

# UNIT 2
# SUNSET ON THE BRITISH EMPIRE
大英帝国の夜明け

 **Prepare to discuss and share your opinion**

イギリスの海外領土はいくつあるだろうか。その中で日が沈まない場所はあるだろうか。

## Vocabulary

Look up the following words and phrases in a dictionary.

| | | | | |
|---|---|---|---|---|
| span | arbitrary | remnant | territory | descendant |
| mutineer | eclipse | convict | streak | millennia |

When (if ever) did the Sun finally set on the British Empire?

—Kurt Amundson

( ANSWER )

 **Reading** ●   📶 Audio 1-03

**1** IT HASN'T YET. BUT only because of a few dozen people living in an area smaller than Disney World.

**The world's largest empire**

**2** The British Empire spanned the globe. This led to the saying that the Sun never set on it, since it was always daytime somewhere in the Empire.    5

**3** It's hard to figure out exactly when this long daylight began. The whole

9

process of claiming a colony (on land already occupied by other people) is awfully arbitrary in the first place. Essentially, The British built their empire by sailing around and sticking flags on random beaches. This makes it hard to decide when a particular spot in a country was "officially" added to the Empire.

*"What about that shadowy place over there?" "That's France. We'll get it one of these days."*

**4** The exact day when the Sun stopped setting on the Empire was probably sometime in the late 1700s or early 1800s, when the first Australian territories were added.

**5** The Empire largely disintegrated in the early 20th century, but — surprisingly — the Sun hasn't technically started setting on it again.

**Fourteen territories**

**6** Britain has 14 overseas territories, the direct remnants of the British Empire.

**7** Many newly independent British colonies joined the Commonwealth of Nations. Some of them, like Canada and Australia, have Queen Elizabeth as their official monarch. However, they are independent states that happen to have the same queen; they are not part of any empire [▷ That they know of.].

**8** The Sun never sets on all 14 British territories at once (or even 13, if you don't count the British Antarctic Territory). However, if the UK loses one tiny territory, it will experience its first Empire-wide sunset in over two centuries.

**9** Every night, around midnight GMT, the Sun sets on the Cayman Islands, and doesn't rise over the British Indian Ocean Territory until after 1:00 A.M.

For that hour, the little Pitcairn Islands in the South Pacific are the only British territory in the Sun. 35

**10** The Pitcairn Islands have a population of a few dozen people, the descendants of the mutineers from the HMS *Bounty*. The islands became notorious in 2004 when a third of the adult male population, including a mayor, were convicted of child sexual abuse.

**11** As awful as the islands may be, they remain part of the British Empire, 40 and unless they're kicked out, the two-century-long British daylight will continue.

## Will it last *forever*?

**12** Well, maybe. In April of 2432, the island will experience its first total solar eclipse since the mutineers arrived. 45

**13** Luckily for the Empire, the eclipse happens at a time when the Sun is over the Cayman Islands in the Caribbean. Those areas won't see a total eclipse; the Sun will even still be shining in London.

**14** In fact, no total eclipse for the next thousand years will pass over the Pitcairn 50 Islands at the right time of day to end the streak. If the UK keeps its current territories and borders, it can stretch out the daylight for a long, long time.

**15** But not forever. Eventually — many 55 millennia in the future — an eclipse will come for the island, and the Sun will finally set on the British Empire.

---

### Notes

**1 Disney World** Walt Disney World Resort のこと。アメリカ合衆国フロリダ州オーランド南西に位置する。

**2 the British Empire** 大英帝国。かつてのイギリスとその植民地、保護領、自治領などの海外領土を含む領土の総称。全盛期には全世界の陸地と人口の4分の1を版図に収めた史上最大の面積を誇り、保有領土のいずれかで必ず太陽が昇っていることから、"the empire on which the sun never sets"（「太陽の沈まない国」）と呼ばれた。

**7 Commonwealth of Nations** イギリス連邦。かつての大英帝国から独立した諸国から構成されるゆるやかな連合体。

**8 the British Antarctic Territory** イギリス領南極地域。イギリスが領有を主張している南極の地域。

**9 GMT** Greenwich Mean Time の略。グリニッジ標準時。　**Cayman Islands** ケイマン諸島。ジャマイカの北西に位置し、グランドケイマン島・ケイマンブラック島・リトルケイマン島の三島からなる。　**Pitcairn Islands** ピトケアン諸島。南太平洋に位置するイギリスの海外領土。無人島であったが、1789年に英国軍艦バウンティ号（HMS *Bounty*）で反乱が起き、反乱者とそのタヒチ人家族が1790年から住みついた（「バウンティ号の反乱」）。

**10 child sexual abuse** 児童性的虐待

**13 the Caribbean** カリブ海

**Comprehension Check**

 **A** Read the sentences below and choose T(true) or F(false).

1. The Sun finally set on the British Empire because of a few dozen people living in an area smaller than Disney World. **T / F**

2. The expansion of the British Empire led to the saying that the Sun never set on it, since it was always daytime somewhere in the Empire. **T / F**

3. The British Empire enforced border security in the early 20th century. **T / F**

4. The Cayman islands have a notorious reputation in 2004 when a third of the adult male population, including a mayor, were convicted of child sexual abuse. **T / F**

5. As long as the Pitcairn islands remain part of the British Empire, the two-century-long British daylight will not last. **T / F**

**B** Select the best answer for each question.

1. In Paragraph 10-15, the author claims that
   (A) the two-century-long British daylight will not continue, because the islands became notorious in 2004 when a third of the adult male population, including a mayor, were convicted of child sexual abuse.
   (B) every night, around midnight GMT, the Sun sets on the Cayman Islands, and doesn't rise over the British Indian Ocean Territory until after 1:00 A.M. Meanwhile, the little Pitcairn Islands in the South Pacific are the only British territory in the Sun.
   (C) no total eclipse for the next thousand years will pass over the Pitcairn Islands at the right time of day to end the streak. If the UK enforced its border security, it can stretch out the daylight for a long, long time.
   (D) the solar eclipse happens at a time when the Sun is over the Pitcairn Islands in the South Pacific. Those areas won't see a total eclipse, while the Sun will even still be shining in London.

2. The expression "figure out" in Paragraph 3 is closest in meaning to
   (A) neglect
   (B) ascertain
   (C) guess
   (D) overlook

3. The word "convict" in Paragraph 10 is closest in meaning to
   (A) surrender
   (B) discharge
   (C) release
   (D) condemn

4. The expression "kicked out" in Paragraph 11 is closest in meaning to
   (A) refuse
   (B) retreat
   (C) expel
   (D) keep

# Writing a Summary

**A** Determine the main idea of the following keywords.

1. Commonwealth of Nations


2. colony


3. GMT


4. solar eclipse


**B** Summarize the passage in about 100 words.

_____

_____

_____

_____

_____

_____

# Discussion

Discuss and share your opinion on "sunset on Japan".

# UNIT 3
# SOUL MATES

ソウルメイト

 **Prepare to discuss and share your opinion**

ソウルメイト（魂の伴侶）は存在するのだろうか。存在するとして、出会うことはできる
だろうか。

 **Vocabulary**

Look up the following words and phrases in a dictionary.

| | | | | |
|---|---|---|---|---|
| statically | assign | assume | odds | vary |
| potential | prominently | model | proverbial | encounter |

**What if everyone actually had only one soul mate, a random person somewhere in the world?**

—Benjamin Staffin

ANSWER

 **Reading** ———————————————————— 🔊 Audio 1-04

**1** WHAT A NIGHTMARE THAT would be.

**2** There are a lot of problems with the concept of a single random soul mate.
As Tim Minchin put it in his song "If I Didn't Have You":

> *Your love is one in a million;*
> *You couldn't buy it at any price.*
> *But of the 9.999 hundred thousand other loves,*
> *Statistically, some of them would be equally nice.*

5

**3** But what if we did have one randomly assigned perfect soul mate, and we *couldn't* be happy with anyone else? Would we find each other?

**4** We'll assume your soul mate is chosen at birth. You don't know anything 10 about who or where they are, but — as in the romantic cliché — you recognize each other the moment your eyes meet.

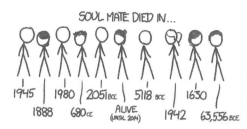

SOUL MATE DIED IN...

1945 | 1980 | 2051 BCE | 5118 BCE | 1630 |
1888  680 CE  ALIVE (UNTIL 2014)  1942  63,556 BCE

**5** Right away, this would raise a few questions. For starters, would your soul mate even still be alive? A hundred 15 billion or so humans have ever lived, but only seven billion are alive now (which gives the human condition a 93 percent mortality rate). If we were all paired up at random, 90 percent of our soul mates would be long dead. 20

**6** That sounds horrible. But wait, it gets worse: A simple argument shows we can't limit ourselves just to past humans; we have to include an unknown number of future humans as well. See, if your soul mate is in the distant past, then it also has to be possible for soul mates to be in the distant future. After all, *your* soul mate's soul mate is. 25

**7** So let's assume your soul mate lives at the same time as you. Furthermore, to keep things from getting creepy, we'll assume they're within a few years of your age. (This is stricter than the standard age-gap creepiness formula [▷ xkcd, "Dating pools," http://xkcd.com/314], but if we assume a 30-year-old and a 40-year-old can be soul mates, then the creepiness rule 30 is violated if they accidentally meet 15 years earlier.) With the same-age restriction, most of us would have a pool of around half a billion potential matches.

**8** But what about gender and sexual orientation? And culture? And language? We could keep using demographics to try to narrow things down 35 further, but we'd be drifting away from the idea of a random soul mate. In our scenario, you wouldn't know *anything* about who your soul mate was until you looked into their eyes. Everybody would have only one orientation: toward their soul mate.

**9** The odds of running into your soul mate would be incredibly small. The 40 number of strangers we make eye contact with each day can vary from almost none (shut-ins or people in small towns) to many thousands (a police officer in Times Square), but let's suppose you lock eyes with an average

of a few dozen new strangers each day. (I'm
45 pretty introverted, so for me that's definitely a
generous estimate.) If 10 percent of them are
close to your age, that would be around 50,000
people in a lifetime. Given that you have
500,000,000 potential soul mates, it means
50 you would find true love only in one lifetime
out of 10,000.

**10** With the threat of dying alone looming so
prominently, society could restructure to try
to enable as much eye contact as possible. We
55 could put together massive conveyor belts to
move lines of people past each other...but if the eye contact effect works over
webcams, we could just use a modified version of ChatRoulette.

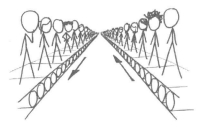

**11** If everyone used the system for eight hours a day,
seven days a week, and if it takes you a couple of seconds
60 to decide if someone's your soul mate, this system
could — in theory — match everyone up with their soul
mates in a few decades. (I modeled a few simple systems

to estimate how quickly people would pair off and drop out of the singles
pool. If you want to try to work through the math for a particular setup, you
65 might start by looking at derangement problems.)

**12** In the real world, many people have trouble finding any time at all for
romance — few could devote two decades to it. So maybe only rich kids would
be able to afford to sit around on SoulMateRoulette. Unfortunately, for the
proverbial 1 percent, most of their soul mates would be found in the other 99
70 percent. If only 1 percent of the wealthy used the service, then 1 percent of
the 1 percent would find their match through this system — one in 10,000.

**13** The other 99 percent of the 1 percent [▷ "We are the zero point nine nine percent!"]
would have an incentive to get more people into the system. They might

sponsor charitable projects to get computers to the rest of the world — a cross between One Laptop Per Child and OKCupid. Careers like "cashier" and "police officer in Times Square" would become high-status prizes because of the eye contact potential. People would flock to cities and public gathering places to find love — just as they do now.

**14** But even if a bunch of us spent years on SoulMateRoulette, another bunch of us managed to hold jobs that offered constant eye contact with strangers, and the rest of us just hoped for luck, only a small minority of us would ever find true love. The rest of us would be out of luck.

**15** Given all the stress and pressure, some people would fake it. They'd want to join the club, so they'd get together with another lonely person and stage a fake soul mate encounter. They'd marry, hide their relationship problems, and struggle to present a happy face to their friends and family. A world of random soul mates would be a lonely one. Let's hope that's not what we live in.

---

**Notes**

**2** Tim Minchin オーストラリア人のコメディアン、俳優、歌手。

**4** romantic cliché 恋愛における陳腐な決まり文句

**7** the standard age-gap creepiness formula デートしても気味悪がられない年齢差の公式

**8** gender and sexual orientation （社会的）性別と性的志向。身体的な性別を意味する "sex" に対し、"gender" は社会的・文化的に形成された性のことを指す。　demographics 人口統計学

**10** conveyor belts ベルト・コンベヤー　ChatRoulette チャット・ルーレット（無作為に抽出された利用者どうしがビデオチャットを行なうウェブサービス）

**11** derangement problems 攪乱順列の問題。数字の並びを完全に攪乱する（元と同じ場所になる要素がない）順列のこと。

**13** One Laptop Per Child 「すべての子どもにパソコンを」という理念に基づき、発展途上国など貧しい国の子どもたちにパソコンを1人1台届けることを目指すNPO団体。　OKCupid アメリカのSNS／出会い系サイト　Times Square タイムズスクエア。アメリカ合衆国、ニューヨーク市最大の繁華街。

## Comprehension Check

 **A** Read the sentences below and choose T(true) or F(false).

1. If we were all linked together at random, 90 percent of our soul mates would be long dead. **T / F**

2. If your soul mate is in the not so distant past, then it also has to be possible for soul mates to be in the present time. **T / F**

3. Despite the same-age restriction, most of us would have a pool of around 500 million potential matches. **T / F**

4. Provided that you have half a billion potential soul mates, it means you would find true love only in one lifetime out of 10,000. **T / F**

5. Even if a bunch of us spent years on SoulMateRoulette, another bunch of us managed to hold jobs that offered constant eye contact with strangers, and the rest of us just hoped for luck, most of us would find true love. **T / F**

**B** Select the best answer for each question.

1. In Paragraph 10-15, the author claims that
   (A) society should restructure to enable as much eye contact as possible because of the threat of dying alone looming so prominently.
   (B) many people can't find any time at all for romance, so they could devote two decades to it in the real world.
   (C) the other 99 percent of the 1 percent of the wealthy would have an incentive to get more people into the SoulMateRoulette.
   (D) a world of random soul mates would be a happy one.

2. The expression "paired up" in Paragraph 5 is closest in meaning to
   (A) put together
   (B) combine
   (C) divine
   (D) pop up

3. The expression "given" in Paragraph 9 is closest in meaning to
   (A) accustomed
   (B) conspiring
   (C) addicted
   (D) considering

4. The word "struggle to" in Paragraph 15 is closest in meaning to
   (A) straight to
   (B) fight to
   (C) forget to
   (D) strive to

## ✎ Writing a Summary

**A** Determine the main idea of the following keywords.

1. cliché

2. gender and sexual orientation

3. restructure

4. SoulMateRoulette

**B** Summarize the passage in about 100 words.

_____

_____

_____

_____

_____

_____

## 😊 Discussion

Discuss and share your opinion on "Reincarnation".

# UNIT 4 EVERYBODY JUMP

みんなでジャンプ

## ⚙ Prepare to discuss and share your opinion

地球上の人類全員がいっせいにジャンプしたら何が起こるだろう。

## 🔤 Vocabulary

Look up the following words and phrases in a dictionary.

| | | | | |
|---|---|---|---|---|
| specific | overweigh | dissipate | compatible | collapse |
| unprecedented | equation | commandeer | engulf | pristine |

**What would happen if everyone on Earth stood as close to each other as they could and jumped, everyone landing on the ground at the same instant?**

—Thomas Bennett (and many others)

ANSWER

## 📖 Reading ────────────────────────── 🔊 Audio 1-05

**1** THIS IS ONE OF the most popular questions submitted through my website. It's been examined before, including by *ScienceBlogs* and *The Straight Dope*. They cover the kinematics pretty well. However, they don't tell the whole story.

5　**2** Let's take a closer look. At the start of the scenario, the entire Earth's  population has been magically transported together into one place.

**3** This crowd takes up an area the size of Rhode Island. But there's no reason to use the vague phrase "an area the size of Rhode Island." This is our scenario; we can be specific. They're *actually* in Rhode Island.　10

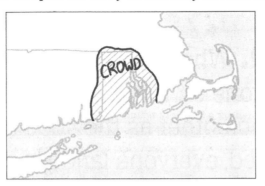

**4** At the stroke of noon, everyone jumps.

**5** As discussed elsewhere, it doesn't really affect the planet. Earth outweighs us by a factor of over ten trillion. On average, we humans can vertically jump maybe half a meter on a good day. Even if the earth were rigid and responded instantly, it would be pushed down by less than an　15 atom's width.

**6** Next, everyone falls back to the ground.

**7** Technically, this delivers a lot of energy into the Earth, but it's spread out over a large enough area that it doesn't do much more than leave footprints in a lot of gardens. A slight pulse of pressure spreads through the North　20 American continental crust and dissipates with little effect. The sound of all those feet hitting the ground creates a loud, drawn-out roar lasting many seconds. Eventually, the air grows quiet.

**8** Seconds pass. Everyone looks around.

25 **9** There are a lot of uncomfortable glances. Someone coughs.

**10** A cell phone comes out of a pocket. Within seconds, the rest of the world's five billion phones follow. All of them — even those compatible with region's towers — are displaying some version of "NO SIGNAL." The cell networks have all collapsed under the unprecedented load. Outside Rhode Island,
30 abandoned machinery begins grinding to a halt.

**11** The T.F. Green Airport in Warwick, Rhode Island, handles a few thousand passengers a day. Assuming they got things organized (including sending out scouting missions to retrieve fuel), they could run at 500 percent capacity for years without making a dent in the crowd.

35 **12** The addition of all the nearby airports doesn't change the equation much. Nor does the region's light rail system. Crowds climb on board container ships in the deep-water port of Providence, but stocking sufficient food and water for a long sea voyage proves a challenge.

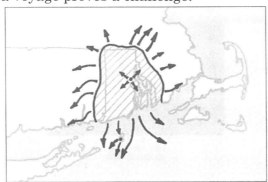

**13** Rhode Island's half-million cars are commandeered. Moments later, I-95,
40 I-195, and I-295 become the sites of the largest traffic jam in the history of the planet. Most of the cars are engulfed by the crowds, but a lucky few get out and begin wandering the abandoned road network.

**14** Some make it past New York or Boston before running out of fuel. Since the electricity is probably not on at this point, rather than find a working
45 gas pump, it's easier to just abandon the car and steal a new one. Who can stop you? All the cops are in Rhode Island.

**15** The edge of the crowd spreads outward into southern Massachusetts and

Connecticut. Any two people who meet are unlikely to have a language in common, and almost nobody knows the area. The state becomes a chaotic patchwork of coalescing and collapsing social hierarchies. Violence is 50 common. Everybody is hungry and thirsty. Grocery stores are emptied. Fresh water is hard to come by and there's no efficient system for distributing it.

🔟 Within weeks, Rhode Island is a graveyard of billions. The survivors spread out across the face of the world and struggle to build a new civilization atop the pristine ruins of the old. Our species staggers on, but 55 our population has been greatly reduced. Earth's orbit is completely unaffected — it spins along exactly as it did before our species-wide jump. But at least now we know.

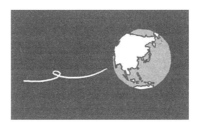

## Notes

**1** *ScienceBlogs* and *The Straight Dope* アメリカの有名な科学記事のブログ・サイト。  **kinematics** 運動学

**3** Rhode Island アメリカ合衆国ロードアイランド州。全米 50 州の中で面積最小の州（4,002 km²）である。

**5** rigid 剛体の（形容詞）。力の作用の下で変形しない物体のこと。  **an atom's width** 原子 1 個分

**7** a slight pulse of pressure わずかなパルス状の圧力  **North American continental crust** 北米大陸の地殻

**10** cell networks 携帯電話のネットワーク

**11** T.F. Green Airport ロードアイランド州中部ケント郡にある空港。州都プロビデンスの南郊約10km、ウォリック市に立地する。

**12** region's light rail system 路面電車を含む地方都市の旅客鉄道  **deep-water port** 深水港  **Providence** プロビデンス。ロードアイランド州の州都。

**13** I-95, I-195, and I-295 州間高速道路 I-95、I-195、I-295

**15** southern Massachusetts and Connecticut マサチューセッツ州南部とコネチカット州  **social hierarchy** 社会階層

##  Comprehension Check

**A** Read the sentences below and choose T(true) or F(false).

1. Jumping on the Earth doesn't really affect the planet, because Earth overweighs us by a factor of over ten trillion. **T / F**

2. Technically, the energy into the Earth is spread out over a large enough area that it can only leave footprints in a lot of gardens. **T / F**

3. Assuming the T. F. Green Airport in Warwick got things organized (including sending out scouting missions to retrieve fuel), they could run at 500 percent capacity for years without making a dent in the crowd. **T / F**

4. Even if Rhode Island became a chaotic patchwork of coalescing and collapsing social hierarchies, Earth's orbit could completely unaffected. **T / F**

5. The survivors spread out across the face of the world and struggle to build a new civilization atop the pristine ruins of the old, but our population has hardly been reduced. **T / F**

**B** Select the best answer for each question.

1. In Paragraph 1-7, the author claims that
   (A) our species can horizontally jump maybe half a meter on a good day.
   (B) a slight pulse of pressure spreads through the North American continental crust and dissipates with little effect.
   (C) it's easier to just abandon the car and steal a new one rather than find a working gas pump if there is the electricity in Providence.
   (D) Earth's orbit would be completely unaffected by our jumping in Rhode Island.

2. The expression "drawn-out" in Paragraph 7 is closest in meaning to
   (A) hush
   (B) long
   (C) short
   (D) calm

3. The expression "come by" in Paragraph 15 is closest in meaning to
   (A) get
   (B) come
   (C) go
   (D) give

4. The expression "stagger on" in Paragraph 16 is closest in meaning to
(A) move away
(B) fix with
(C) walk around
(D) survive through

## ✎ Writing a Summary

**A** Determine the main idea of the following keywords.

1. rigid (object)

2. Providence

3. social hierarchy

4. civilization

**B** Summarize the passage in about 100 words.

_____

_____

_____

_____

_____

_____

## 😀💬 Discussion

Discuss and share your opinion on "jumping on the moon".

# UNIT 5
# A MOLE OF MOLES

1モルのモグラ

 **Prepare to discuss and share your opinion**

モグラ（mole）を一か所に 1 モル（mole）集めたら、どうなるだろうか。

ABC **Vocabulary**

Look up the following words and phrases in a dictionary.

> gruesome    definition    trillion    smother    integrity  uniformly
> lukewarm    decompose    sterilize    insulate    surpass

**What would happen if you were to gather a mole (unit of measurement) of moles (the small furry critter) in one place?**

—Sean Rice

ANSWER

 **Reading** ━━━━━━━━━━━━━━━━━━━━━━━━━━━ 📶 Audio 1-06

**1** THINGS GET A BIT gruesome.

**2** First, some definitions. A mole is a unit. It's not a typical unit, though. It's really just a number — like "dozen" or "billion." If you have a mole of something, it means you have

5  602,214,129,000,000,000,000,000 of them (usually written $6.022 \times 10^{23}$). It's such a big number [▷ "One mole" is close to the number of atoms in a gram of hydrogen. It's also, by chance, a decent ballpark guess for the number of grains of sand on Earth.] because

THERE ARE TOO MANY MOLECULES.

it's used for counting numbers of molecules, which there are a lot of. 10

**3** A mole is also a type of burrowing mammal. There are handful of types of moles, and some of them are truly horrifying [ ▷ http://en.wikipedia.org/wiki/File:Condylura.jpg]. 15

**4** So what would a mole of moles — 602,214,129,000,000,000,000,000 animals — look like?

**5** First, let's start with wild approximations. This is an example of what might go through my head before I even pick up a calculator, when I'm just trying to get a sense of the quantities — the kind of calculation where 10,1, 20 and 0.1 are all close enough that we can consider them equal:

**6** A mole (the animal) is small enough for me to pick up and throw. [citation needed] Anything I can throw weighs 1 pound. One pound is 1 kilogram. The number 602,214,129,000,000,000,000,000 looks about twice as long as a trillion, which means it's about a trillion trillion. I happen to remember that 25 a trillion trillion kilograms is how much a planet weighs.

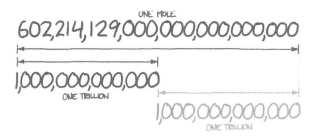

*...If anyone asks, I did not tell you it was okay to do math like this.*

**7** That's enough to tell us that we're talking about a pile of moles on the scale of a planet. It's a pretty rough estimate, since it could be off by a factor of thousands in either direction.

**8** Let's get some better numbers. An eastern mole (*Scalopus aquaticus*) 30 weighs about 75 grams, which means a mole of moles weighs:

$$(6.022 \times 10^{23}) \times 75g \approx 4.52 \times 10^{22} kg$$

**9** That's a little over half the mass of our moon. Mammals are largely water. A kilogram of water takes up a liter of volume, so if the moles weigh $4.52 \times 10^{22}$ kilograms, they take up about $4.52 \times 10^{22}$ liters of volume. You 35 might notice that we're ignoring the pockets of space between the moles. In a moment, you'll see why.

**10** The cube root of $4.52 \times 10^{22}$ liters is 3562 kilometers, which means we're talking about a sphere with a radius of 2210 kilometers, or a cube 2213
40  miles on each edge.[1]

**11** If these moles were released onto the Earth's surface, they'd fill it up to 80 kilometers deep — just about to the (former) edge of space:

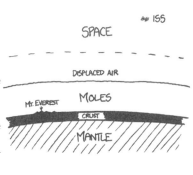

**12** This smothering ocean of high-pressure
45  meat would wipe out most life on the planet, which could — to reddit's horror — threaten the integrity of the DNS system. So doing this on Earth is definitely not an option.

**13** Instead, let's gather the moles in interplanetary space. Gravitational
50  attraction would pull them into a sphere. Meat doesn't compress very well, so it would undergo only a little bit of gravitational contraction, and we'd end up with a mole planet slightly larger than the Moon.

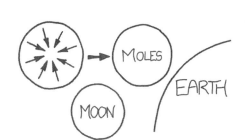

**14** The moles would have a surface gravity of about one-sixteen of
55  Earth's — similar to that of Pluto. The planet would start off uniformly lukewarm — probably a bit over room temperature — and the gravitational contraction would heat the deep
60  interior by a handful of degrees.

**15** But this is where it gets weird. The mole planet would be a giant sphere of meat. It would have a lot of latent energy (there are enough calories in the mole planet to support the Earth's current population for 30 billion years). Normally, when organic matter decomposes, it releases much of that energy
65  as heat. But throughout the majority of the planet's interior, the pressure would be over 100 megapascals, which is high enough to kill all bacteria and sterilize the mole remains — leaving no microorganisms to break down the mole tissue.

**16** Closer to the surface, where the pressure would be lower, there would
70  be another obstacle to decomposition — the interior of a mole planet would be low in oxygen. Without oxygen, the usual decomposition couldn't

happen, and the only bacteria that would be able to break down the moles would be those that don't require oxygen. While inefficient, this anaerobic decomposition can unlock quite a bit of heat. If continued unchecked, it would heat the planet to a boil. 75

**17** But the decomposition would be self-limiting. Few bacteria can survive at temperatures above about 60℃, so as the temperature went up, the bacteria would die off, and the decomposition would slow. Throughout the planet, the mole bodies would gradually break down into kerogen, a mush of organic matter that would — if the planet were hotter — eventually form oil. 80

**18** The outer surface of the planet would radiate heat into space and freeze. Because the moles form a literal fur coat, when frozen they would insulate the interior of the planet and slow the loss of heat to space. However, the flow of heat in the liquid interior would be dominated by convection. Plumes of hot meat and bubbles of trapped gases like methane — along with the air 85 from the lungs of the deceased moles — would periodically rise through the mole crust and erupt volcanically from the surface, a geyser of death blasting mole bodies free of the planet.

**19** Eventually, after centuries of millennia of turmoil, the planet would calm and cool enough that it would begin to freeze all the way through, The deep 90 interior would be under such high pressure that as it cooled, the water would crystalize out into exotic forms of ice such as ice III and ice V, and eventually ice II and ice IX [ ▷ No relation.].

**20** All told, this is a pretty bleak picture. Fortunately, there's a better approach. I don't have any reliable numbers for global mole population (or 95 small mammal biomass in general), but we'll take a shot in the dark and estimate that there are at least a few dozen mice, rats, vole, and other small mammals for every human.

**21** There might be a billion habitable planets in our galaxy. If we colonized them, we'd certainly bring mice and rats with us. If just one in a hundred 100 were populated with small mammals in numbers similar to Earth's, after a few million years — not long, in evolutionary time — the total number that have ever lived would surpass Avogadro's number. If you want a mole of moles, build a spaceship.

## Notes

**8** *Scalopus aquaticus* トウブモグラ

**10** cube root 立方根  radius 半径

**12** high-pressure 高圧の  reddit's horror ソーシャル・ニュース・サイトの reddit が、ネット上の著作権侵害行為の防止法案によって DNS 機能を阻害する措置が可能になったことに抗議したことを踏まえたジョーク。  **DNS system** ドメイン・ネーム・システム。インターネット上でドメイン名とＩＰアドレスの対応関係を管理するシステム。

**13** gravitational attraction 重力、万有引力  gravitational contraction 重力収縮

**14** surface gravity 表面重力  Pluto 冥王星

**15** latent energy 潜在エネルギー  organic matter 有機物  microorganism 微生物

**16** decomposition 分解  oxygen 酸素

**17** self-limiting 自己制御的  kerogen ケロゲン

**18** bubbles of trapped gases 拘束された気体の泡  methane メタン  a geyser of death 死の間欠泉

**20** biomass 一定の空間に存在する動植物すべてを有機物として換算した量  mice, rats, vole ハツカネズミ、クマネズミ、ハタネズミ

**21** Avogadro's number アボガドロ数。１モルの純物質中に存在する分子の数。

 **Comprehension Check**

**A** Read the sentences below and choose T(true) or F(false).

1. The number 602,214,129,000,000,000,000,000 looks about twice as long as a trillion, which equals it's about a trillion trillion. **T / F**

2. If the moles weigh $4.52 \times 10^{22}$ kilograms, they take up about $4.52 \times 10^{22}$ liters of volume. **T / F**

3. This smothering ocean of high-pressure meat would help most life on the planet, which could ensure the integrity of the DNS system. **T / F**

4. Without oxygen, the usual decomposition couldn't happen, and the only bacteria that would be able to break down the moles would be those that require kerogen. **T / F**

5. If just 1% of habitable planets were populated with small mammals in numbers similar to Earth's, after a few million years the total number that ever lived would surpass Avogadro's number. **T / F**

**B** Select the best answer for each question.

1. In Paragraph 15-21, the author claims that
   (A) the mole planet would have a lot of latent energy, which releases much of that energy as heat when organic matter decomposes.
   (B) although the decomposition would be self-limiting, bacteria can survive at temperatures above about 60℃, so as the temperature went up, the bacteria would die of.

(C) plumes of hot meat and bubbles of trapped gases like Kerogen would rarely rise through the mole crust and erupt volcanically from the surface.

(D) the small mammals that have ever lived would surpass Avogadro's number, and then we could build a spaceship made by a mole of moles.

2. The word "compress" in Paragraph 13 is closest in meaning to
   (A) strengthen
   (B) lengthen
   (C) shorten
   (D) stretch

3. The word "unchecked" in Paragraph 16 is closest in meaning to
   (A) controlled
   (B) reasonable
   (C) restrained
   (D) unbridled

4. The expression "break down into" in Paragraph 17 is closest in meaning to
   (A) decompose
   (B) put together
   (C) develop
   (D) bring together

 ## Writing a Summary

 **A**  Determine the main idea of the following keywords.

1. mammal

2. surface gravity

3. decomposition

4. self-limiting

**B** Summarize the passage in about 100 words.

_____

_____

_____

_____

_____

_____

## Discussion

Discuss and share your opinion on "building a spaceship".

# UNIT 6
# MACHINE-GUN
# JETPACK
マシンガン・ジェットパック

 **Prepare to discuss and share your opinion**

マシンガンでジェットパックを作って下向きに発射させたら、飛べるのだろうか。

## 🔤 Vocabulary

Look up the following words and phrases in a dictionary.

| | | | | |
|---|---|---|---|---|
| bullet | recoil | tape down | ideally | spit out |
| irrelevant | magazine | standstill | inflict | brace |

## Is it possible to build a jetpack using downward-firing machine guns?

—Rob B

Q

ANSWER

 **Reading** ────────────────────────── 🔊 Audio 1-07

**1** I WAS SORT OF surprised to find that the answer was yes! But to really do it right, you'll want to talk to the Russians.

**2** The principle here is pretty simple. If you fire a bullet forward, the recoil pushes you back. So if you fire downward, the recoil should push you up.

**3** The first question we have to answer is "can a gun even lift its own 5 weight?" If a machine gun weighs 10 pounds but produces only 8 pounds of recoil when firing, it won't be able to lift itself off the ground, let alone lift itself plus a person.

**4** In the engineering world, the ratio between a craft's thrust and the weight is called, appropriately, thrust-to-weight ratio. If it's less than 1, the vehicle can't lift off. The *Saturn V* had a takeoff thrust-to-weight ratio of about 1.5.

**5** Despite growing up in the South, I'm not really a firearms expert, so to help answer this question, I got in touch with an acquaintance in Texas.[1] Note: Please, PLEASE do not try this at home.

**6** As it turns out, the AK-47 has a thrust-to-weight ratio of around 2. This means if you stood it on end and somehow taped down the trigger, it would rise into the air while firing.

SATURN V       KALASHNIKOV XLVII

**7** This isn't true of all machine guns. The M60, for example, probably can't produce enough recoil to lift itself off the ground.

**8** The amount of thrust created by a rocket (or firing machine gun) depends on (1) how much mass it's throwing out behind it, and (2) how fast it's throwing it. Thrust is the product of these two amounts:

**9** Thrust = Mass ejection rate × Speed of ejection

**10** If an AK-47 fires ten 8-gram bullets per second at 715 meters per second, its thrust is:

$$10 \ \tfrac{\text{bullets}}{\text{second}} \times 8 \ \tfrac{\text{grams}}{\text{bullet}} \times 715 \ \tfrac{\text{meters}}{\text{second}} = 57.2\text{N} \approx 13 \text{ pounds of force}$$

**11** Since the AK-47 weighs only 10.5 pounds when loaded, it should be able to take off and accelerate upward.

**12** In practice, the actual thrust would turn out to be up to around 30 percent higher. The reason for this is that the gun isn't spitting out just bullets — it's also spitting out hot gas and explosive debris. The amount of extra force this adds varies by gun and cartridge.

**13** The overall efficiency also depends on whether you eject the shell casings out of the vehicle or carry them with you. I asked my Texan acquaintances if they could weigh some shell casings for my calculations. When they had trouble finding a scale, I helpfully suggested that given the size of their arsenal, really they just need to find someone *else* who owned a scale [▷ Ideally someone with less ammo.].

**14** So what does all this mean for our jetpack? Well, the AK-47 could take off, but it doesn't have enough spare thrust to lift anything weighing much more than a squirrel.

**15** We can try using multiple guns. If you fire two guns at the ground, it creates twice the thrust. If each gun can lift 5 pounds more than its own weight, two can lift 10. At this point, it's clear where we're headed:

*You will not go to space today.*

**16** If we add enough rifles, the weight of the passenger becomes irrelevant;

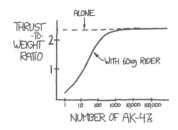

it's spread over so many guns that each one barely notices. As the number of rifles increases, since the contraption is effectively many individual rifles flying in parallel, the craft's thrust-to-weight ratio approaches that of a single, unburdened rifle: But there's a problem: ammunition.

**17** An AK-47 magazine holds 30 rounds. At 10 rounds per second, this would provide a measly three seconds of acceleration.

**18** We can improve this with a larger magazine — but only up to a point. It turns out there's no advantage to carrying more than about 250 rounds of ammunition. The reason for this is a fundamental and central problem in rocket science: Fuel makes you heavier.

**19** Each bullet weighs 8 grams, and the cartridge (the "whole bullet") weighs over 16 grams. If we added more than about 250 rounds, the AK-47 would be too heavy to take off.

**20** This suggests our optimal craft would comprise a large number of AK-47s (a minimum of 25 but ideally at least 300) carrying 250 rounds of ammunition each. The largest versions of this craft could accelerate upward to vertical speeds approaching 100 meters per second, climbing over half a kilometer into the air.

**21** So we've answered Rob's question. With enough machine guns, you could fly. But our AK-47 rig is clearly not a practical jetpack. Can we do better?

**22** My Texas friends suggested a series of machine guns, and I ran the numbers on each one. Some did pretty well; the MG-42, a heavier machine gun, had a marginally higher thrust-to-weight ratio than the AK-47. Then
75 we went bigger.

**23** The GAU-8 Avenger fires up to 60 1-pound bullets a *second*. It produces almost 5 tons of recoil force, which is crazy considering that it's mounted in a type of plane (the A-10 "Warthog") whose two engines produce only 4 tons of thrust each. If you put two of them, in one aircraft, and fired both
80 guns forward while opening up the throttle, the guns would win and you'd accelerate backward.

**24** To put it another way: If I mounted a GAU-8 on my car, put the car in neutral, and started firing backward from a standstill, I would be breaking interstate speed limit in less than *three seconds*.

85 **25** As good as this gun would be as a rocket pack engine, the Russians built one that would work even better. The Gryazev-Shipunov GSh-6-30 weighs half as much as the GAU-8 and has an even higher fire
90 rate. Its thrust-to-weight ratio approaches

*"Actually what I'm confused about is how."*

40, which means if you pointed one at the ground and fired, not only would it take off in a rapidly expanding spray of deadly metal fragments, but you would experience 40 gees of acceleration.

**26** This is way too much. In fact, even when it was firmly mounted in an
95 aircraft, the acceleration was a problem:

**27** *[T]he recoil... still had a tendency to inflict damage on the aircraft. The rate of fire was reduced to 4,000 rounds a minute but it didn't help much. Landing lights almost always broke after firing...Firing more than about 30 rounds in a burst was asking for trouble from overhearting...*

100
— Greg Goebel, airvectors.net

**28** But if you somehow braced the human rider, made the craft strong enough to survive the acceleration, wrapped the GSh-6-30 in an aerodynamic shell, and made
105 sure it was adequately cooled......you could jump mountains.

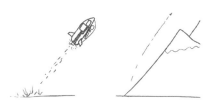

## Notes

**4 thrust** 推力　**thrust-to-weight ratio** 推力重量比　*Saturn V* サターンⅤ型ロケット。アメリカ合衆国のアポロ計画およびスカイラブ計画で使用された、使い捨て方式の液体燃料多段式ロケット。

**6 AK-47** カラシニコフ自動小銃 AK-47

**7 M60** M60 機関銃

**9 mass ejection rate** 一定時間あたりに放出する質量　**Speed of ejection** 放出の速度

**12 cartridge** カートリッジ。弾頭（弾丸）、ケース（薬きょう）、パウダー（火薬）、プライマー（雷管）で構成される弾薬筒（実包）のこと。

**13 shell casings** 薬きょう　**arsenal** 貯蔵武器

**17 magazine** 弾倉

**18 rocket science** ロケット科学

**19 whole bullet** 実包、実弾。

**20 ammunition** 弾薬。連発銃などの補充用の弾丸をこめておく部分。　**vertical speeds** 垂直速度

**22 MG-42** グロスフス MG42 機関銃

**23 GAU-8 Avenger** GAU-8 アベンジャー機関砲　**A-10 "Warthog"** アメリカ空軍の攻撃機 A-10「ウォートホッグ」

**24 interstate speed limit** 州間高速道路の制限速度

**25 Gryazev-Shipunov GSh-6-30** グリアゼフ＝シプノフ GSh-6-30

**28 an aerodynamic shell** 空気力学的に設計された保護版

 # Comprehension Check

### A Read the sentences below and choose T(true) or F(false).

1. If you stood the AK-47 on end and somehow taped down the trigger, it would rise into the air while firing.　　　　**T / F**

2. The AK-47 should be impossible to take off and accelerate upward, it weighs 10.5 pounds when loaded.　　　　**T / F**

3. The AK-47 could take off, and also it has enough spare thrust to lift anything weighing much more than a squirrel.　　　　**T / F**

4. The GAU-8 Avenger produces almost 5 tons of recoil force, which is crazy considering that it's mounted in a type of plane whose two engines produce only 4 tons of thrust each.　　　　**T / F**

5. If you somehow braced the human rider, made the craft strong enough to survive the acceleration, wrapped the GSh-6-30 in an aerodynamic shell, and made sure it was adequately cooled, you could jump mountains.　　　　**T / F**

**B** Select the best answer for each question.

1. In Paragraph 8-28, the author claims that
   (A) the amount of thrust created by the AK47 is independent of how much mass its throwing out behind it, and how fast it's throwing it.
   (B) by adding enough rifles, the weight of the passenger becomes more important; it's spread over so many guns that each one notices.
   (C) if you put two of GAU-8, in one aircraft, and fired both guns forward while opening up the throttle, the guns would win and you'd accelerate backward.
   (D) GSh-6-30 would take off in a rapidly expanding spray of deadly metal fragments, but you would never experience 40 gees of acceleration.

2. The word "acquaintance" in Paragraph 5 is closest in meaning to
   (A) ignorance
   (B) friend
   (C) enemy
   (D) acquittance

3. The word "practical" in Paragraph 21 is closest in meaning to
   (A) skilled
   (B) incompetent
   (C) efficient
   (D) pragmatic

4. The word "mounted" in Paragraph 23 is closest in meaning to
   (A) isolated
   (B) detached
   (C) installed
   (D) removed

 **Writing a Summary**

 Determine the main idea of the following keywords.

1. thrust


2. thrust-to-weight ratio

**3.** cartridge

**4.** the GAU-8 Avenger

 Summarize the passage in about 100 words.

_____

_____

_____

_____

_____

_____

## Discussion

Discuss and share your opinion on "hydrogen peroxide-powered rocket packs".

# UNIT 7
# RISING STEADILY

昇り続ける

 **Prepare to discuss and share your opinion**

秒速１フィート（30 センチ）で空に向かって昇り続けたら、どうなるだろうか。

[ABC] **Vocabulary**

Look up the following words and phrases in a dictionary.

| | | | | |
|---|---|---|---|---|
| steadier | pop | measurably | chilly | frostbite |
| succumb | symptom | interstellar | hypothetical | consume |

If you suddenly began rising steadily at 1 foot per second, how exactly would you die? Would you freeze or suffocate first? Or something else?

—Rebecca B

(ANSWER)

 **Reading** ————————————— 🔊 Audio 1-08

**1** DID YOU BRING A COAT?

**2** A foot per second isn't that fast; it's substantially slower than a typical elevator. It would take you 5-7 seconds to rise out of arm's reach, depending how tall
5  your friends are.

**3** After 30 seconds, you'd be 30 feet — 9 meters — off the ground. If you skip ahead to page 168, you'll learn

that this is your last chance for a friend to throw you a sandwich or water bottle or something [▷ It won't help you survive, but…].

**4** After a minute or two, you would be above the trees. For the most part, you'd still be about as comfortable as you were on the ground. If it's a breezy day, it would probably get chillier thanks to the steadier wind above the tree line [ ▷ For this answer, I'm going to assume a typical atmosphere

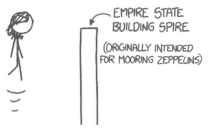

EMPIRE STATE BUILDING SPIRE

(ORIGINALLY INTENDED FOR MOORING ZEPPELINS)

temperature profile. It can, of course, vary quite a bit.] .

**5** After 10 minutes you would be above all but the tallest skyscrapers, and after 25 minutes you'd pass the spire of the Empire State Building.

**6** The air at these heights is about 3 percent thinner than it is at the surface. Fortunately, your body handles air pressure changes like that all the time. Your ears might pop, but you wouldn't really notice anything else.

**7** Air pressure changes quickly with height. Surprisingly, when you're standing on the ground, air pressure changes measurably within just a few feet. If you phone has a barometer in it, as a lot of modern phones do, you can download an app and actually see the pressure difference between your head and your feet.

**8** A foot per second is pretty close to a kilometer per hour, so after an hour, you'll be about a kilometer off the ground. At this point, you definitely start to get chilly. If you have a coat, you'll still be OK, though you might also notice the wind picking up.

**9** At about two hours and two kilometers, the temperature would drop below freezing. The wind would also, most likely, be picking up. If you have any exposed skin, this is where frostbite would start to become a concern.

**10** At this point, the air pressure would fall below what you'd experience in an airliner cabin [▷ …which are typically kept pressurized at 70 percent to 80 percent of sea level pressure, judging from the barometer in my phone.], and the effects would start to become more significant. However, unless you had a warm coat, the temperature would be a bigger problem.

**11** Over the next two hours, the air would drop to below-zero temperatures. Assuming for a moment that you survived the oxygen deprivation, at some point you'd succumb to hypothermia. But when? [ ▷ Either unit.] [ ▷ Not Kelvin, though.]

**12** The scholarly authorities on freezing to death seem to be, unsurprisingly, Canadians. The most widely used model for human survival in cold air was developed by Peter Tikuisis and John Frim for the Defence and Civil Institute of Environmental Medicine in Ontario.

**13** According to their model, the main factor in the cause of death would be your clothes. If you were nude, you'd probably succumb to hypothermia somewhere around the five-hour mark, before your oxygen ran out [ ▷ And frankly, this "nude" scenario raises more questions than it answers.]. If you were bundled up, you may be frostbitten, but you would probably survive…long enough to reach the Death Zone.

**14** Above 8,000 meters — above the tops of all but the highest mountains — the oxygen content in the air is too low to support human life. Near this zone, you would experience a range of symptoms, possibly including confusion, dizziness, clumsiness, impaired vision, and nausea.

**15** As you approach the Death Zone, your blood oxygen content would plummet. Your veins are supposed to bring low-oxygen blood back to your lungs to be refilled with oxygen. But in the Death Zone, there's so little oxygen in the air that your veins lose oxygen to the air instead of gaining it.

**16** The result would be a rapid loss of consciousness and death. This would happen around the seven-hour mark; the chances are very slim that you would make it to eight.

*She died as she lived—rising at a foot per second.*
*I mean, as she lived for the last few hours.*

**17** And two million years later, your frozen body, still moving along steadily at a foot per second, would pass through the heliopause into interstellar space.

**18** Clyde Tombaugh, the astronomer who discovered Pluto, died in 1997. A portion of his remains were placed on the *New Horizons* spacecraft, which will fly past Pluto and then continue out of the solar system.

**19** It's true that your hypothetical foot-per-second trip would be cold, 75
unpleasant, and rapidly fatal. But when the Sun becomes a red giant in four
billion years and consumes the Earth, you and Clyde would be the only ones
to escape. So there's that.

**Notes**

**5** skyscrapers 超高層ビル  **Empire State Building** アメリカ合衆国ニューヨーク州ニューヨーク市マンハッタン区にある超高層ビル

**10** airliner cabin 旅客機の客室

**11** below-zero temperatures 氷点下の気温  **either unit** 華氏でも摂氏でも  **kelvin** ケルビン（絶対温度の単位）
oxygen deprivation 酸素欠乏  **hypothermia** 低体温症

**12** the scholarly authorities 学術研究の権威者
**the Defence and Civil Institute of Environmental Medicine in Ontario** カナダのオンタリオ州にある医薬環境局

**13** Death Zone デスゾーン。人間が生存できないほど酸素濃度が低い高所の領域を指す登山用語。

**14** impaired vision 視覚障害  **nausea** 吐き気

**15** blood oxygen 血中酸素量

**17** heliopause ヘリオポーズ。太陽から噴き出す太陽風とそれに伴う磁場が、銀河系の星間物質とその磁場にぶつかって形成する境界面。その内側の太陽風が届く範囲を太陽圏と呼ぶ。

**18** Clyde Tombaugh クライド・トンボー。1930 年に冥王星を発見した業績で特に知られているアメリカの天文学者。
*New Horizons* spacecraft 宇宙船ニューホライズンズ。NASA が 2006 年に打ち上げた人類初の冥王星を含む太陽系外縁天体の探査を行なう無人探査機。

**Comprehension Check**

 Read the sentences below and choose T(true) or F(false).

1. If it's a rainy day, it would probably get chillier thanks to the steadier wind above the tree line.                                                          **T / F**

2. Near the Death Zone, you would experience a range of symptoms, possibly including confusion, dizziness, clumsiness, impaired vision, and nausea.    **T / F**

3. In the Death Zone, there's a little oxygen in the air that your veins lose oxygen to the air without gaining it.                                      **T / F**

4. Clyde's ashes were placed on the New Horizons spacecraft, which will fly past Pluto and then continue out of the solar system.                        **T / F**

5. Although you and Clyde would never escape from the hypothetical foot-per-second trip, the Sun becomes a red giant in four billion years and consumes the Earth.  **T / F**

**B** Select the best answer for each question.

1. In Paragraph 10-16, the author claims that
   (A) the air pressure in an airliner cabin is unable to remain pressurized at 70 percent to 80 percent of sea level pressure, judging from a professional barometer.
   (B) the temperature would drop below zero at about two hours and two kilometers, and the effects would start to become more significant unless you had a warm coat.
   (C) the main factor in the cause of death would be your clothes as Peter Tikuisis and John Frim for the Defence and Civil Institute of Environmental Medicine in Ontario proposed for the model for human survival in cold air.
   (D) your blood oxygen content would increase, and our veins are supposed to bring low-oxygen blood back to your lungs to be refilled with oxygen if you approach the Death Zone.

2. The word "pop" in Paragraph 6 is closest in meaning to
   (A) rising
   (B) ringing
   (C) singing
   (D) beating

3. The expression "ran out" in Paragraph 13 is closest in meaning to
   (A) filled
   (B) existed

(C) supplied
(D) exhausted

4. The expression "bundled up" in Paragraph 13 is closest in meaning to
   (A) wear
   (B) bunch
   (C) assemble
   (D) disrobe

## ✏ Writing a Summary

**A** Determine the main idea of the following keywords.

1. Hypothermia

2. frostbite

3. Death Zone

4. heliopause

**B** Summarize the passage in about 100 words.

_____

_____

_____

_____

_____

_____

## 😊💬 Discussion

Discuss and share your opinion on "turning steadily".

# UNIT 8
# ORBITAL
# SUBMARINE
軌道上の潜水艦

 **Prepare to discuss and share your opinion** ────────○

潜水艦を軌道上に打ち上げたら、どうなるだろうか。

📇ABC **Vocabulary** ─────────────────────────────○

Look up the following words and phrases in a dictionary.

| | | | | |
|---|---|---|---|---|
| seal | manufacture | pedantic | absorb | livable |
| propel | tumble | crevice | deceleration | disable |

## How long could a nuclear submarine last in orbit?

—Jason Lathbury

(ANSWER)

 **Reading** ──────────────────────────── 🔊 Audio 1-09

**1** THE SUBMARINE WOULD BE fine, but the crew would be in trouble.

**2** The submarine wouldn't burst. Submarine hulls are strong enough to withstand 50 to 80 atmospheres of external pressure from water, so they'd have no problem containing 1 atmosphere of internal pressure from air.

5 **3** The hull would likely be airtight. Although watertight seals don't necessarily hold back air, the fact that water can't find a way through the hull under 50 atmospheres of pressure suggests that air won't escape

quickly. There may be a few specialized one-way valves that would let air out, but in all likelihood, the submarine would remain sealed.

**4** The big problem the crew would face would be the obvious one: air. Nuclear submarines use electricity to extract oxygen from water. In space, there's no water,[citation needed] so they wouldn't be able to manufacture more air. They carry enough oxygen in reserve to survive for a few days, at least, but eventually they'd be in trouble.

**5** To stay warm, they could run their reactor, but they'd have to be very careful how *much* they ran it — because the ocean is colder than space.

**6** Technically, that's not really true. Everyone knows that space is very cold. The reason spacecraft can overheat is that space isn't as thermally conductive as water, so heat builds up more quickly in spacecraft than in boats. But if you're even *more* pedantic, it *is* true. The ocean is colder than space.

**7** Interstellar space is very cold, but space near the Sun — and near Earth — is actually incredibly hot! The reason it doesn't seem that way is that in space, the definition of "temperature" breaks down a little bit. Space seems cold because it's so *empty*.

**8** Temperature is a measure of the average kinetic energy of a collection of particles. In space, individual molecules have a high average kinetic energy, but there are so few of them that they don't affect you.

**9** When I was a kid, my dad had a machine shop in our basement, and I remember watching him use a metal grinder. Whenever metal touched the grinding wheel, sparks flew everywhere, showering his hands and clothes. I couldn't understand why they didn't hurt him — after all, the growing sparks were several thousand degrees.

DAD, WHY DON'T THE SPARKS BURN YOU?

WELL, SON, I HAVE A MUTATION THAT MAKES ME HEAL RAPIDLY, AND I HAVE AN ADAMANTIUM-REINFORCED SKELETON—

YOU'RE DESCRIBING WOLVERINE.

NO, PRETTY SURE THAT'S ME.

**10** I later learned that the reason the sparks didn't hurt him was that they were *tiny*; the heat they carried could be absorbed into the body without warming anything more than a tiny patch of skin.

**11** The hot molecules in space are like the sparks in my dad's machine shop; they might be hot or cold, but they're so small that touching them doesn't change your temperature much.[1] Instead, your heating and cooling is dominated by how much heat you produce and how quickly it pours out of you into the void.

45 **12** Without a warm environment around you radiating heat back to you, you lose heat by radiation much faster than normal. But without air around you to carry heat from your surface, you also don't lose much heat by convection [ ▷ Or conduction.]. For most human-carrying spacecraft, the latter effect is more important; the big problem isn't staying warm, it's keeping cool.

50 **13** A nuclear submarine is clearly able to maintain a livable temperature inside when the outer hull is cooled to 4℃ by the ocean. However, if the submarine's hull needed to hold this temperature while in space, it would lose heat at a rate of about 6 megawatts while in the shadow of the Earth. This is more than the 20 kilowatts supplied by the crew — and the few
55 hundred kilowatts of apricity [ ▷ This is my single favorite word in the English language. It means the warmth of sunlight in winter.] when in direct sunlight — so they'd need to run the reactor just to stay warm [ ▷ When they moved into the Sun, the sub's surface warm, but they'd still be losing heat faster than they'd be gaining it.].

WAIT, WHAT DO YOU MEAN, "WITHOUT ROCKETS"?

60 **14** To get out of orbit, a submarine would need to slow down enough that it hit the atmosphere. Without rockets, it has no way to do this. Okay — technically, a submarine *does* have rockets.

**15** Unfortunately, the rockets are pointing
65 the wrong way to give the submarine a push. Rockets are self-propelling, which means they have very little recoil. When a gun fires a bullet, it's *pushing* the bullet up to speed. With a rocket, you just light it and let go. Launching
70 missiles won't propel a submarine forward. But *not* launching them could.

WEIRD HOW THE SMOKE IS BILLOWING IN A VACUUM. SHHH.

**16** If the ballistic missiles carried by a modern nuclear submarine were taken from their tubes, turned around, and placed in the tubes backward, they
75 could each change the submarine's speed by about 4 meters per second.

**17** A typical de-orbiting maneuver requires in the neighborhood of 100 m/s of delta-v (speed change), which means that the 24 Trident missiles carried by an *Ohio*-class submarine could be just enough to get it out of orbit.

**18** Now, because the submarine has no heat-dissipating ablative tiles, and

because it's not aerodynamically stable at hypersonic velocities, it would   80
inevitably tumble and break up in the air.

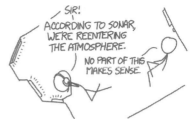

**19** If you tucked yourself into the right crevice in the submarine — and were
strapped into an acceleration couch — there's a tiny, tiny, *tiny* chance that
you could survive the rapid deceleration. Then you'd need to jump out of the
wreckage with a parachute before it hit the ground.   85

**20** If you ever try this, and I suggest you
don't, I have one piece of advice that is
absolutely critical: Remember to disable
the detonators on the missiles.

---

### Notes

**2** submarine hull  潜水艦の船殻

**3** airtight  気密性のある   watertight seal  水密を保つためのシール材

**4** nuclear submarine  原子力潜水艦   citation needed  要出典。ウィキペディアにおいて信頼できる情報源が出典として求められていることを編集者が示すときの言葉。

**5** reactor  原子炉

**6** thermally conductive  熱伝導性の

**8** kinetic energy  運動エネルギー   a collection of particles  粒子の集合体   individual molecules  個々の分子

**9** metal grinder  金属研削機   grinding wheel  研削盤の砥石車

**12** convection  対流。熱せられた流体が上部へ移動し、周囲の低温の流体が流れ込むことを繰り返す現象。
human-carrying spacecraft  有人宇宙船

**15** self-propelling  自力で進む

**16** ballistic missiles  弾道ミサイル

**17** de-orbiting maneuver  軌道離脱マヌーバ   delta-v  軌道の変更に必要な速度変化   24 Trident missiles  24 発搭載のトライデント・ミサイル   *Ohio*-class submarine  オハイオ級原子力潜水艦。アメリカ海軍が現在保有する唯一の戦略ミサイル原子力潜水艦。

**18** heat-dissipating ablative tile  熱を逃す耐熱タイル   hypersonic velocity  極超音速（度）

**19** acceleration couch  高速カウチ。『スターウォーズ』等のＳＦ映画に登場する宇宙船に搭載された加速度を相殺できるシートのこと。

**20** detonator  起爆装置

**Comprehension Check** ─────────────────────────────────

**A** Read the sentences below and choose T(true) or F(false).

1. Submarine hulls are too strong to withstand 50 to 80 atmospheres of external pressure from water, so they'd have a problem containing 1 atmosphere of internal pressure from air.                                         **T / F**

2. Nuclear submarines carry enough oxygen in reserve to survive for a few days, at least, but eventually they'd be in trouble.                                   **T / F**

3. Interstellar space is very cold, but space near the Sun is actually incredibly hot; though for it doesn't seem like it would be that way in space, the definition of "temperature" breaks down a little bit.                                   **T / F**

4. Regardless of heat or cold, the hot molecules in space are so small that touching them doesn't change your temperature much. Instead, your heating and cooling depends on how much heat you produce.                                   **T / F**

5. The nuclear submarine would be under control because the submarine has heat-dissipating ablative tiles, and because it's aerodynamically stable at hypersonic velocities.                                   **T / F**

**B** Select the best answer for each question.

1. In Paragraph 8-20, the author claims that
   (A) individual molecules are so small that touching them doesn't change your temperature much because they have high average kinetic energy in space.
   (B) you lose much heat by convection, with a warm environment around you radiating heat back to you.
   (C) a nuclear submarine would clearly be able to maintain a livable temperature inside when the submarine's hull needs to hold this temperature in space.
   (D) there's a small chance that you could survive the rapid deceleration if you tucked yourself into the right crevice in the submarine and were strapped into an acceleration couch.

2. The word "in all likelihood" in Paragraph 3 is closest in meaning to
   (A) unlikely
   (B) probably
   (C) improbable
   (D) unbelievable

3. The word "strapped" in Paragraph 19 is closest in meaning to
   (A) hang
   (B) suspend

(C) belt

(D) remove

4.  The word "critical" in Paragraph 20 is closest in meaning to

(A) crucial

(B) optional

(C) trivial

(D) superficial

## ✏️ Writing a Summary

**A** Determine the main idea of the following keywords.

1. thermally conductivity

2. kinetic energy

3. convection

4. de-orbiting maneuver

**B** Summarize the passage in about 100 words.

_____

_____

_____

_____

_____

_____

## 😀 Discussion

Discuss and share your opinion on "orbital satellite".

# UNIT 9
# LITTLE PLANET

星の王子さまの惑星

 **Prepare to discuss and share your opinion** ●

「星の王子さま」が住む惑星が実際にあったとしたら、どんな惑星だろうか。

 **Vocabulary**

Look up the following words and phrases in a dictionary.

| | | | | |
|---|---|---|---|---|
| asteroid | poignant | memorable | ostensibly | solidify |
| parable | superdense | weird | elongate | chaotically |

If an asteroid was very small but supermassive, could you really live on it like the Little Prince?

—Samantha Harper

*"Did you eat my rose?" "Maybe."*

ANSWER

 **Reading**

**1** *THE LITTLE PRINCE*, BY Antoine de Saint-Exupéry, is a story about a traveler from a distant asteroid. It's simple and sad and poignant and memorable.[1] It's ostensibly a children's book, but it's hard to pin down who the intended audience is. In any case, it certainly *has* found an audience; it's among the best-selling books in history. 5

**2** It was written in 1942. That's an interesting time to write about asteroids, because in 1942 we didn't actually know what asteroids *looked* like. Even in our best telescopes, the largest *asteroids* were visible only as points of light. In fact, that's where their name comes from — the 10 word *asteroid* means "starlike."

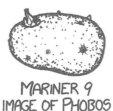

MARINER 9
IMAGE OF PHOBOS

**3** We got our first confirmation of what asteroids looked like in 1971, when *Mariner 9* visited Mars and snapped pictures of Phobos and Deimos. These moons, believed to be captured asteroids, solidified the modern image of 15 asteroids as cratered potatoes.

**4** Before the 1970s, it was common for science fiction to assume small asteroids would be round, like planets.

**5** *The Little Prince* took this a step further, imagining an asteroid as a tiny planet with gravity, air, and a rose. There's no point in trying to critique the 20 science here, because (1) it's not a story about asteroids, and (2) it opens with a parable about how foolish adults are for looking at everything too literally.

**6** Rather than using science to chip away at the story, let's see what strange new pieces it can add. If there really were a superdense asteroid with enough surface gravity to walk around on, it would have some pretty remarkable 25 properties.

**7** If the asteroid had a radius 1.75 meters, them in order to have Earthlike gravity at the surface, it would need to have a mass of about 500 million tons. This is roughly equal to the combined mass of every human on Earth.

**8** If you stood on the surface, you'd experience tidal forces. Your feet 30 would feel heavier than your head, which you'd feel as a gentle stretching sensation. It would feel like you were stretched out on a curved rubber ball, or were lying on a merry-go-round with your head near the center.

**9** The escape velocity at the surface would be about 5 meters per second. That's slower than a sprint, but still pretty fast. As a rule of thumb, if you 35

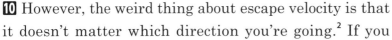

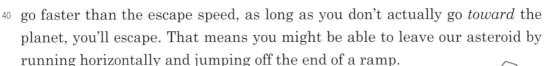

can't dunk a basketball, you wouldn't be able to escape this asteroid by jumping.

**10** However, the weird thing about escape velocity is that it doesn't matter which direction you're going.[2] If you go faster than the escape speed, as long as you don't actually go *toward* the planet, you'll escape. That means you might be able to leave our asteroid by running horizontally and jumping off the end of a ramp.

**11** If you didn't go fast enough to escape the planet, you'd go into orbit around it. Your orbital speed would be roughly 3 meters per second, which is a typical jogging speed. But this would be a *weird* orbit.

**12** Tidal forces would act on you in several ways. If you stretched your arm down toward the planet, it would be pulled much harder than the rest of you. And when you reach down with one arm, the rest of you gets pushed upward, which means other parts of your body feel even *less* gravity. Effectively, every part of your body would be trying to go in a different orbit.

**13** A large orbiting object under these kinds of tidal forces — say, a moon — will generally break apart into rings [ ▷ This is presumably what happened to Sonic the Hedgehog.]. This wouldn't happen to you. However, your orbit would become chaotic and unstable.

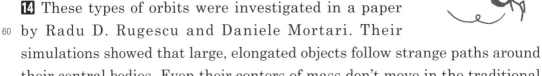

**14** These types of orbits were investigated in a paper by Radu D. Rugescu and Daniele Mortari. Their simulations showed that large, elongated objects follow strange paths around their central bodies. Even their centers of mass don't move in the traditional ellipses; some adopt pentagonal orbits, while others tumble chaotically and crash into the planet.

**15** This type of analysis could actually have practical applications. There have been various proposals over the years to use long, whirling tethers to move cargo in and out of gravity wells — a sort of free-floating space elevator. Such tethers could transport cargo to and from the surface of the Moon, or to pick up space-craft from the edge of the Earth's atmosphere. The inherent instability of many tether orbits poses a challenge for such a project. As for the residents of our superdense asteroid, they'd have to be careful; if they ran too fast, they'd be in serious danger of entering orbit, going into a tumble and losing their lunch. Fortunately, vertical jumps would be fine.

*Cleveland-area fans of French children's literature were disappointed by the Prince's decision to sign with the Miami Heat.*

---

### Notes

**❶** *The Little Prince*, **by Antoine de Saint-Exupéry**　フランス人の小説家アントワーヌ・ド・サン＝テグジュペリ (1900-44) の『星の王子さま』(1943)。

**❸** *Mariner 9*　マリナー９号。NASA のマリナー計画の火星探査機。　　**Phobos and Deimos**　フォボスとダイモス。フォボスが火星の第一衛星。第二衛星であるダイモスより大きく、より内側の軌道を回っている。

**❻** **superdense asteroid**　超高密度小惑星

**❽** **tidal force**　潮汐（ちょうせき）力。重力によって起こる二次的効果の一種で、潮汐の原因になる力。

**❾** **escape velocity**　宇宙速度。天体の表面から打ち上げられた物体を宇宙空間に飛び出させるのに必要な最小発射速度。

**⓭** **Sonic the Hedgehog**　セガグループのビデオゲームに登場するキャラクター

**⓮** **Radu D. Rugescu and Daniele Mortari**　ラドゥ・D・ルゲスクとダニエル・モルタリ。ルーマニアの科学者。 **central bodies**　中心天体

**⓯** **gravity well**　重力井戸。天体が周辺に作る重力場の形を井戸に喩えている。　　**space elevator**　宇宙（軌道）エレベータ。惑星などの表面から静止軌道以上まで伸びる軌道を持つエレベータ。　　**Cleveland-area**　クリーブランド地区。アメリカ合衆国オハイオ州北東部に位置する。　　**Miami Heat**　マイアミ・ヒート。アメリカ合衆国フロリダ州マイアミに本拠を置く全米プロバスケットボール協会 (NBA) のチーム。

## Comprehension Check

 **A** Read the sentences below and choose T(true) or F(false).

1. *The Little Prince* is ostensibly a children's book, but it's hard to determine who the intended audience is. **T / F**

2. In *The Little Prince*, the author images an asteroid as a tiny planet with gravity, air, and a rose, but we would try to critique the science here. **T / F**

3. The escape velocity speed would be roughly 3 meters per second, which is a typical running speed, but this would be a *weird* orbit. **T / F**

4. Even if a large orbiting object under these kinds of tidal forces would generally break up, your orbit wouldn't become chaotic and unstable. **T / F**

5. There have been various projects over the years to use long, whirling tethers to move cargo in and out of gravity wells — a sort of free-floating space elevator. **T / F**

**B** Select the best answer for each question.

1. In Paragraph 12-15, the author claims that
   (A) tidal forces would act on you in several ways if you stretched your arm down toward the planet and pulled much harder than the rest of you.
   (B) the inherent instability of many tether wouldn't happen to your space-craft, because of tidal forces.
   (C) the tethers for space elevator could transport cargo to and from the surface of the Moon, or to pick up space-craft from the edge of the Earth's atmosphere.
   (D) the residents of our superdense asteroid would be in serious danger of entering orbit, if they weren't be careful.

2. The expression "chip away at" in Paragraph 6 is closest in meaning to
   (A) underestimate
   (B) support
   (C) undermine
   (D) build

3. The expression "As a rule of thumb" in Paragraph 9 is closest in meaning to
   (A) according to rule
   (B) thumb through
   (C) roughly speaking
   (D) thumb on the scale

4.  The expression "break apart" in Paragraph 13 is closest in meaning to
    (A) fade away
    (B) divide into
    (C) combine with
    (D) break down

## ✏ Writing a Summary

**A** Determine the main idea of the following keywords.

1.  asteroid

2.  tidal force

3.  escape velocity

4.  space elevator

**B** Summarize the passage in about 100 words.

_____

_____

_____

_____

_____

_____

## 😀 Discussion

Discuss and share your opinion on "space elevator".

# UNIT 10
# COMMON COLD

風邪

 **Prepare to discuss and share your opinion** ────────●

風邪に感染しない方法はあるのだろうか。

ABC **Vocabulary** ─────────────────────────────────●

Look up the following words and phrases in a dictionary.

| | | | | |
|---|---|---|---|---|
| culprit | immunity | quarantine | reasonable | linger |
| die out | unravel | conceivably | eradicate | vaccine |

If everyone on the planet stayed away from each other for a couple of weeks, wouldn't the common cold be wiped out?

—Sarah Ewart

(ANSWER)

 **Reading** ────────────────────────────── 📶 Audio 2-02

**1** WOULD IT BE WORTH IT?

**2** The common cold is caused by a variety of viruses [▷ "Virii" is used occasionally but discouraged. "Viræ" is definitely wrong.], but rhinoviruses are the most

5   common culprit [▷ Any upper respiratory infection can actually be the cause of the "common cold."]. These viruses take over the cells in your nose and throat and use them to produce more viruses.

After a few days, your immune system notices and destroys it, [ ▷ The immune response is actually the cause of your symptoms, not the virus itself.] but not before you infect, on average, one other person [ ▷ Mathematically, this must be true. If the average were less than one, the virus would die out. If it were more than one, eventually everyone would have a cold all the time.].  After you fight off the infection, you are immune to that particular rhinovirus strain — an immunity that lasts for years.

**3** If Sarah put us all in quarantine, the cold viruses we carry would have no fresh hosts to run to. Could our immune systems then wipe out every copy of the virus?

**4** Before we answer that question, let's consider the practical consequences of this kind of quarantine. The world's total annual economic output is in the neighborhood of $80 trillion, which suggests that interrupting all economic activity for a few weeks would cost many trillions of dollars. The shock to the system from the worldwide "pause" could easily cause a global economic collapse.

**5** The world's total food reserves are probably large enough to cover us for four or five weeks of quarantine, but the food would have to be evenly parceled out beforehand. Frankly, I'm not sure what I'd do with a 20-day grain reserve while standing alone in a field somewhere.

**6** A global quarantine brings us to another question: How far apart can we actually *get* from one another? The world is big, [citation needed] but there are a lot of people.[citation needed]

**7** If we divide up the world's land area evenly, there's enough room for each of us to have a little over 2 hectares each, with the nearest person 77 meters away.

**8** While 77 meters is probably enough separation to block the transmission of rhinoviruses, that separation would come at a cost. Much of the world's land is not pleasant to stand around on for five weeks. A lot of us would be stuck standing in the Sahara Desert [ ▷ 450 million people.], or central Antarctica [ ▷

40 650 million people.].

**9** A more practical — though not necessarily cheaper — solution would be to give everyone biohazard suits. That way, we could walk around and 45 interact, even allowing some normal economic activity to continue:

**10** But let's set aside the practicality and address Sarah's actual question: Would it *work*? To help figure out the answer, I talked to Professor Ian M. Mackay, a virology expert from the Australian Infectious Diseases Research 50 Centre at the University of Queensland [ ▷ I first tried to take the question to *Boing Boing's* Cory Doctorow, but he patiently explained to me that he's not actually a doctor.].

**11** Dr. Mackay said that this idea is actually somewhat reasonable, from a purely biological point of view. He said that rhinoviruses — and other RNA respiratory viruses — are completely eliminated from the body by 55 the immune system; they do not linger after infection. Furthermore, we don't seem to pass any rhinoviruses back and forth with animals, which means there are no other species that can serve as reservoirs of our colds. If rhinoviruses don't have enough humans to move between, they die out.

**12** We've actually seen this viral extinction in action in isolated populations. 60 The remote islands of St. Kilda, far to the northwest of Scotland, for centuries hosted a population of about 100 people. The islands were visited by only a few boats a year, and suffered from an unusual syndrome called the *cnatan-na-gall*, or "stranger's cough." For several centuries, the cough swept the island like clockwork every time a new boat arrived.

65 **13** The exact cause of the outbreaks is unknown,[1] but rhinoviruses were probably responsible for many of them. Every time a boat visited, it would introduce new strains of virus. These strains would sweep the islands, infecting virtually everyone. After several weeks, all the residents would have fresh immunity to those strains, and with nowhere to go, the viruses 70 would die out. The same viral cleaning would likely to happen in any small and isolated population — for example, shipwreck survivors.

**14** If all humans were isolated from one another, the St. Kilda scenario would play out on a species-wide scale. After a week or two, our colds would run their course, and healthy immune systems would have plenty of time 75 to clear the viruses. Unfortunately, there's one catch, and it's enough to unravel the whole plan: We don't all *have* healthy immune systems.

**15** In most people, rhinoviruses are fully cleared from the body within about ten days. The story is different for those with severely weakened immune systems. In transplant patients, for example,

whose immune systems have been artificially suppressed, common infections — including rhinoviruses — can linger for 85 weeks, months, or conceivably years.

**16** This small group of immunocompromised people would serve as safe havens for rhinoviruses. The hope of eradicating them is slim; they would need to survive in only a few hosts in order to sweep out and 90 retake the world.

**17** In addition to probably causing the collapse of civilization, Sarah's plan wouldn't eradicate rhinoviruses [ ▷ Unless we ran out of food during the quarantine and all starved to death; in that case, human rhinoviruses would die with us.]. However, this might be for the best! 95

**18** While colds are no fun, their absence might be worse. In his book *A Planet of Viruses*, author Carl Zimmer says that children who aren't exposed to rhinoviruses have more immune disorders as adults. It's possible that these mild infections serve to train and calibrate our immune systems.

**19** On the other hand, colds suck. And in addition to being unpleasant, some 100 research says infections by these viruses also *weaken* our immune systems directly and can open us up to further infections.

**20** All in all, I wouldn't stand in the middle of a desert for five weeks to rid

myself of colds forever. But if they ever come up with a rhinovirus vaccine, I'll
115  be first in line.

---

**Notes**

**2 immune system** 免疫系。生体内で病原体などの非自己物質やがん細胞などの異常な細胞を認識して殺滅することにより、生体を病気から保護する多数の機構が集積したシステム。 **rhinoviruse** ライノウイルス。風邪の代表的な原因ウイルス。 **rhinovirus strain** ライノウイルス株

**3 host** （寄生動物の）宿主

**4 the world's total annual economic output** 世界経済の年間総生産高

**5 total food reserves** 食料総備蓄量

**8 the Sahara Desert** サハラ砂漠 **Antarctica** 南極

**9 biohazard suit** バイオハザード防護服

**10 virology** ウイルス学 **the Australian Infectious Diseases Research Centre at the University of Queensland** クイーンズランド大学のオーストラリア国立感染症センター **Boing Boing's Cory Doctorow** ブログ Boing Boing の編集者コリイ・ドクトロウ。カナダ人の SF 作家。

**11 biological point of view** 生物学的な観点 **RNA respiratory virus** RNA 呼吸器系ウイルス

**12 St. Kilda** セント・キルダ。北大西洋、ノース・ウイスト島の 64km 西北西にある、イギリス領の孤立した群島。 *cnatan-na-gall* スコットランド語で "stranger's cough(cold)" の意。"boat-cough"（「ボート咳」）とも呼ばれる。

**15 transplant patient** 臓器移植患者

**16 immunocompromised** 免疫無防備状態の

**18 *A Planet of Viruses*** カール・ジンマーの著書『ウイルス・プラネット』(2015) **immune disorder** 免疫異常

**Comprehension Check**

 **A** Read the sentences below and choose T(true) or F(false).

1. When you fight off an infection, you will be immune to that particular rhinovirus strain — an immunity that lasts for years. **T / F**

2. The shock to the immune system suggests that interrupting all economic activity for a few weeks would cost many trillions of dollars. **T / F**

3. As 77 meters is probably enough separation to block the transmission of rhinoviruses, the rest of us would be stuck standing in the Sahara Desert, or central Antarctica. **T / F**

4. In transplant patients common infections can linger for weeks, months, or conceivably years, for their immune systems have been artificially suppressed.

   **T / F**

5. Some research suggests that infections by these viruses not only weaken our immune systems directly but also can open us up to further infections.

   **T / F**

 **B** Select the best answer for each question.

1. In Paragraph 11-18, the author claims that
   (A) rhinoviruses — and other RNA respiratory viruses — are completely eliminated from the body by the immune system; they do not linger after infection.
   (B) the viral cleaning in St. Kilda would likely to happen in any small and isolated population — for example, shipwreck survivors.
   (C) healthy immune systems would have plenty of time to clear the viruses, and hope of eradicating them is possible because they would need to survive in hosts in order to sweep out and retake the world.
   (D) it's possible that these mild infections serve to train and calibrate our immune systems; therefore, children who aren't exposed to rhinoviruses have more immune disorders as adults.

2. The word "culprit" in Paragraph 2 is closest in meaning to
   (A) offender
   (B) cause
   (C) criminal
   (D) guilty

3. The expression "wipe out" in Paragraph 3 is closest in meaning to
   (A) reserve
   (B) scavenge
   (C) remove
   (D) reboot

4. The word "calibrate" in Paragraph 18 is closest in meaning to
   (A) adjust
   (B) disturb
   (C) improve
   (D) diminish

 **Writing a Summary**

**A** Determine the main idea of the following keywords.

1. immune system


2. rhinovirus


3. St. Kilda


4. stranger's cough


**B** Summarize the passage in about 100 words.

_____

_____

_____

_____

_____

_____

**Discussion**

Discuss and share your opinion on "infection".

# UNIT 11
# ALIEN
# ASTRONOMERS
異星人の天文学者

 **Prepare to discuss and share your opinion**

異星人がいるとしたら、地球はどのように見えるだろうか。

**Vocabulary**

Look up the following words and phrases in a dictionary.

| | | | | |
|---|---|---|---|---|
| detectable | transmission | outshine | bounce | monitor |
| obsolete | hypothetical | promising | reflectivity | terraform |

Let's assume that there's life on the nearest habitable exoplanet and that they have technology comparable to ours. If they looked at our star right now, what would they see?

—Chuck H

 **Reading**

🔊 Audio 2-03

**1** Let's try a more complete answer. We'll start with...

**Radio transmissions**

**2** *Contact* popularized the idea of aliens listening in on our broadcast media. Sadly, the odds are against it.

5　**3** Here's the problem: Space is really big. You can work through the physics of interstellar radio attenuation [ ▷ I mean, if you want.], but the problem is captured pretty well by considering the economics of the situation: If your TV signals are getting to another star, you're wasting money. Powering a transmitter is expensive, and creatures on other stars aren't buying the products in the TV
10　commercials that pay your power bill.

**4** The full picture is more complicated, but the bottom line is that as our technology has gotten better, less of our radio traffic has been leaking out into space. We're closing down the giant transmitting antennas and switching to cable, fiber, and tightly focused cell-tower networks.

15　**5** While our TV signals may have been detectable — with great effort — for a while, that window is closing. Even in the late 20th century, when we were using TV and radio to scream into the void at the top of our lungs, the signal probably faded to undetectability after a few light-years. The potentially habitable exoplanets we've spotted so far are dozens of light-years away, so
20　the odds are they aren't currently repeating our catchphrases [ ▷ Contrary to the claims made by certain unreliable webcomics.]. But TV and radio transmissions still weren't Earth's most powerful radio signal. They were outshone by the beams from early-warning radar.

**6** Early-warning radar, a product of the Cold War, consisted of a bunch of
25　ground and airborne stations scattered around the Arctic. These stations swept the atmosphere with powerful radar beams 24/7, often bouncing them off the ionosphere, and people obsessively monitored the echos for any hints of enemy movement [ ▷ I wasn't alive during most of this period, but from what I hear, the mood was tense.].

30　**7** These radar transmissions leaked into space, and could probably be picked up by nearby exoplanets if they happened to be listening when the beam swept over their part of the sky. But the same march of technological progress that made the TV broadcast towers obsolete has had the same effect on early-warning radar. Today's systems — where they exist at all —
35　are much quieter, and may eventually be replaced completely by new

SIR, THE ENEMY HAS LAUNCHED A MISSILE.

HOW DO YOU KNOW?

TWITTER.

technology.

**8** Earth's most *powerful* radio signal is the beam from the Arecibo telescope. This massive dish in Puerto Rico can function as a radar transmitter, bouncing a signal off nearby targets like Mercury and the asteroid belt. It's essentially a flashlight that we shine on planets to see them better. (This is just as crazy as it sounds.)

**9** However, it transmits only occasionally, and in a narrow beam. If an exoplanet happened to be caught in the beam, and they were lucky enough to be pointing a receiving antenna at our corner of the sky at the time, all they would pick up would be a brief pulse of radio energy, then silence [ ▷ Which is exactly what we saw once, in 1977. The source of this blip (dubbed the "Wow Signal") has never been identified.].

**10** So hypothetical aliens looking at Earth probably wouldn't pick us up with radio antennas. But there's also...


**Visible Light**

**11** This is more promising. The Sun is really bright,[citation needed] and its light illuminates the Earth.[citation needed] Some of that light is reflected back into space as "Earthshine." Some of it skims close to our planet and passes through our atmosphere before continuing on to the stars. Both of these effects could potentially be detected from an exoplanet.

**12** They wouldn't tell you anything about humans directly, but if you watched the Earth for long enough, you could figure out a lot about our atmosphere from the reflectivity. You could probably figure out what our water cycle looked like, and our oxygen-rich atmosphere would give you a hint that something weird was going on.

**13** So in the end, the clearest signal from Earth might not be from us at all. It might be from the algae that have been terraforming the planet — and altering the signals we send into space — for billions of years.

*Heeeey, look at the time, Gotta run.*

**14** Of course, if we wanted to send a clearer signal, we could. A radio transmission has the problem that they have to be paying attention when it arrives.

**15** Instead, we could *make* them pay attention. With ion drives, nuclear
70 propulsion, or just clever use of the Sun's gravity well, we could probably send a probe out of the solar system fast enough to reach a given nearby star in a few dozen millennia. If we can figure out how to make a guidance system that survives the trip (which would be tough), we could use it to steer toward any inhabited planet.

75 **16** To land safely, we'd have to slow down. But slowing down takes even more fuel. And, hey, the whole point of this was for then to notice us, right? So maybe if those aliens looked toward our solar system, this is what they would see.

---

**Notes**

**2** *Contact* 1997 年のアメリカ映画。地球外生命体と人類の接触を描いたカール・セーガンによる S F 小説の映画化作品。

**3** **the physics of interstellar radio attenuation** 惑星間の電波減衰についての物理学。星と星のあいだで電波がどの程度弱まるかを理解するための物理学の意。  **transmitter** 送信機  **power bill** 電気料金

**4** **radio traffic** 無線通信（の量）  **transmitting antennas** 送信用アンテナ

**5** **light-years** 光年。天文学で用いられる距離の単位。

**6** **early-warning radar** 早期警戒レーダー  **Cold War** 冷戦  **ground and airborne stations** 地上ステーションと空中ステーション  **ionosphere** 電離層。地球を取り巻く大気の上層部にある分子や原子が、紫外線や X 線などにより電離した領域のこと。この領域は電波を反射する性質を持ち、これによって短波帯の電波を用いた遠距離通信が可能になる。

**7** **exoplanet** 太陽系外惑星  **technological progress** 技術革新

**8** **Arecibo telescope** プエルトリコのアレシボにある米国立天文電離層センター（NAIC）の電波天文台。  **asteroid belt** 小惑星帯。太陽系の中で火星と木星の間にある小惑星の軌道が集中している領域を指す。

**9** **Wow Signal** 1977 年 8 月 15 日に SETI プロジェクトの観測を行なっていたオハイオ州立大学のジェリー・R・エーマンが、ビッグイヤー電波望遠鏡で受信した電波信号。狭い周波数に集中した強い信号で、太陽系外の地球外生命によって送信された可能性が指摘されている。

**11** **Earthshine** 地球照。新月の前後、月の欠けて見える部分が、地球から反射した太陽光に照らされて薄明るく見える現象。

**12** **water cycle** 水循環。地球における継続的な水の循環のこと。  **oxygen-rich atmosphere** 酸素を豊富に含む大気

**13** **algae** 藻類。酸素発生型光合成を行なう生物のうち、地上に生息するシダ、コケ、種子植物を除いたものの総称。

**15** **ion drive** イオン駆動。電気推進と呼ばれる方式を採用したロケットエンジンの一種。  **nuclear propulsion** 原子力推進。原子力をエネルギー源とする推進のこと。  **Sun's gravity well** 太陽の重力井戸。太陽の重力。  **probe** 宇宙探査機。探査機の一種で、地球以外の天体などを探査する目的で地球軌道外の宇宙に送り出される宇宙機のこと。

## ⚛ Comprehension Check

**A**  Read the sentences below and choose T(true) or F(false).

1.  Powering a transmitter is costly, and creatures on other stars aren't buying the products in the TV commercials that pay your power bill.   **T / F**

2.  Early-warning radar's stations swept the atmosphere with powerful radar beams 24/7, often bouncing them off the ionosphere, and people obsessively monitored the echos for any hints of enemy movement.   **T / F**

3.  Today's systems are much quieter, and may eventually be replaced completely by new technology, for the same march of technological progress that made the TV broadcast towers obsolete has had the same effect on early-warning radar.   **T / F**

4.  Some of moonshine skims close to our planet and passes through our atmosphere before continuing on to the stars, while both of these effects could hardly be detected from an exoplanet.   **T / F**

5.  If we can research how to make a guidance system that survives the trip, we could live and survive in any harsh environment toward any inhabited planet.   **T / F**

**B** Select the best answer for each question.

1. In Paragraph 11-16, the author claims that
   (A) we could probably research what our water cycle looked like, and our oxygen-rich atmosphere would give us a hint that something familiar was going on.
   (B) the clearest signal from Earth might be from the algae that have been terraforming the planet — and altering the signals we send into space — for billions of years, which might not be from alien astronomers at all.
   (C) with ion drives, nuclear propulsion, or just clever use of the Sun's gravity well, we could probably launch a spacecraft out of the solar system fast enough to reach a given nearby star in a few dozen millennia.
   (D) we should not slow down safely despite the need for fuel, because the whole point of this was to make us noticeable any inhabited planet and alien astronomers.

2. The expression "closing down" in Paragraph 4 is closest in meaning to
   (A) accepting
   (B) terminating
   (C) employing
   (D) establishing

3. The word "skims" in Paragraph 11 is closest in meaning to
   (A) rushes
   (B) abstains
   (C) pours
   (D) grazes

4. The expression "be detected" in Paragraph 11 is closest in meaning to
   (A) be caught
   (B) be concealed
   (C) be ignored
   (D) be given

  **Writing a Summary**

**A** Determine the main idea of the following keywords.

1. early-warning radar



2. cold war

**3.** earthshine

**4.** water cycle

**B** Summarize the passage in about 100 words.

_____

_____

_____

_____

_____

_____

## Discussion

Discuss and share your opinion on "the nearest habitable exoplanet".

# UNIT 12
# INTERPLANETARY CESSNA
惑星間セスナ

 **Prepare to discuss and share your opinion**

飛行機を太陽系以外の天体の上空で飛ばすことはできるだろうか。

ABC **Vocabulary**

Look up the following words and phrases in a dictionary.

| | | | | |
|---|---|---|---|---|
| undo | pump | vaporize | simulate | launch |
| plow into | hellish | upshot | minimal | adhesive |

What would happen if you tried to fly a normal Earth airplane above different solar system bodies?

—Glen Chiacchieri

ANSWER

 **Reading** ──────────────────────────── 🔊 Audio 2-04

**1** HERE'S OUR AIRCRAFT [ ▷ The Cessna 172 Skyhawk, probably the most common plane in the world.]:

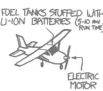

FUEL TANKS STUFFED WITH LI-ION BATTERIES (5-10 mn RUN TIME)

ELECTRIC MOTOR

**2** We have to use an electric motor because gas engines work only near green plants. On worlds without plants, oxygen doesn't stay in the atmosphere — it combines with other elements to form things like carbon dioxide and rust. 5 Plants undo this by stripping the oxygen back out and pumping it into the air. Engines need oxygen in the air to run [ ▷ Also, our gasoline is MADE of ancient plants.].

**3** Here's our pilot:

**4** Here's what would happen if our aircraft were launched above the surface of the 32 largest solar system bodies: 10

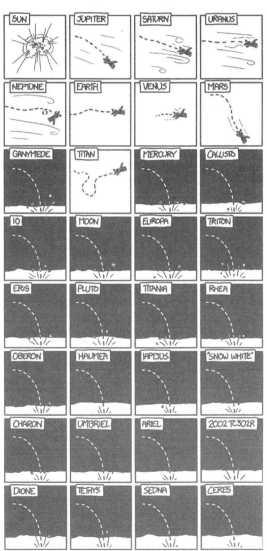

**5** In most cases, there's no atmosphere, and the plane would fall straight to the ground. If it were dropped from 1 kilometer or less, in a few cases the crash would be slow 15 enough that the pilot could survive — although the life-support equipment probably wouldn't.

**6** There are nine solar system bodies with atmospheres thick enough to 20 matter: Earth — obviously — Mars, Venus, the four gas giants, Saturn's moon Titan, and the Sun. Let's take a closer look at what would happen to a plane on each one. 25

**7** **The Sun**: This would work about as well as you'd imagine. If the plane were released close enough to the Sun to feel its atmosphere at all, it would be vaporized in less than a second. 30

**8** **Mars**: To see what would happen to our aircraft on Mars, we turn to X-Plane. X-Plane is the most advanced flight simulator in the world. The

35 product of 20 years of obsessive labor by a hardcore aeronautics enthusiast [▷ Who uses capslock a lot when talking about planes.] and community of supporters, it actually simulates the flow of air over every piece of an aircraft's body as it flies. This makes it a valuable research tool, since it can accurately simulate entirely new aircraft designs — and new environments.

40 **9** In particular, if you change the X-Plane config file to reduce gravity, thin the atmosphere, and shrink the radius of the planet, it can simulate flight on Mars. X-Plane tells us that flight on Mars is difficult, but not impossible. NASA knows this, and has considered surveying Mars by airplane. The tricky thing is that with so little atmosphere, to get any lift, you have to go

45 *fast*. You need to approach Mach 1 just to get off the ground, and once you get moving, you have so much inertia that it's hard to change course — if you turn, your plane rotates, but keeps moving in the original direction. The X-Plane author compared piloting Martian aircraft to flying a supersonic ocean liner.

50 **10** Our Cessna 172 wouldn't be up to the challenge. If launched from 1 km, it wouldn't build up enough speed to pull out of a dive, and would plow into the Martian terrain at over 60 m/s (135 mph). If dropped from 4 or 5 kilometers, it could gain enough speed to pull up into a glide — at over half the speed of sound. The landing would not be survivable.

55 **11 Venus**: Unfortunately, X-Plane is not capable of simulating the hellish environment near the surface of Venus. But physics calculations give us an idea of what flight there would be like. The upshot is: Your plane would fly pretty well, expect it would be on fire the whole time, and then it would stop flying, and then stop being a plane.

60 **12** The atmosphere on Venus is over 60 times denser than Earth's. It's thick enough that a Cessna moving at jogging speed would rise into the air. Unfortunately, that air is hot enough to melt lead. The paint would start melting off in seconds, the plane's components would fail rapidly, and the plane would glide gently into the ground as it came apart under the heat

65 stress.

**13** A much better bet would be to fly above the clouds. While Venus's surface is awful, its upper atmosphere is surprisingly Earthlike. At 55 kilometers, a human could survive with an oxygen mask and protective wetsuit; the air is room temperature and the pressure is similar to that on Earth mountains.

70 You would need the wetsuit, though, to protect you from the sulfuric acid [▷ I'm

not selling this well, am I?].

**14** The acid's no fun, but it turns out the area right above the clouds is a great environment for an airplane, as long as it has no exposed metal to be corroded away by the sulfuric acid. And is capable of flight in constant category-5-hurricane-level winds, which are another thing I forgot to mention earlier. Venus is a terrible place. 75

**15 Jupiter**: Our Cessna wouldn't be able to fly on Jupiter; the gravity is just too strong. The power needed to maintain level flight under Jupiter's gravity is three times greater than that on Earth. Starting from a friendly sea-level pressure, we'd accelerate through the tumbling winds into a 275 m/s (600mph) 80 downward glide deeper and deeper through the layers of ammonia ice and water ice until we and the aircraft were crushed. There's no surface to hit; Jupiter transitions smoothly from gas to liquid as you sink deeper and deeper.

**16 Saturn**: The picture here is a little friendlier than on Jupiter. The weaker gravity — close to Earth's, actually — and slightly denser (but still 85 thin) atmosphere mean that we'd be able to struggle along a bit further before we gave in to either the cold or high winds and descended to the same fate as on Jupiter.

**17 Uranus**: Uranus is a strange, uniform bluish orb. There are high winds and it's bitterly cold. It's the friendliest of the gas giants to our Cessna, and 90 you could probably fly for a little while. But given that it seems to be an almost completely featureless planet, why would you want to?

**18 Neptune**: If you're going to fly around one of the ice giants, I would probably recommend Neptune [ ▷ Motto: "The Slightly Bluer One."] over Uranus. It at least has some clouds to look at before you freeze to death or break apart 95 from the turbulence.

**19 Titan**: We've saved the best for last. When it comes to flying, Titan might be better than Earth. Its atmosphere is thick but its gravity is light, giving it a surface pressure only 50 percent higher than Earth's with air four times as dense. Its gravity — lower than that of the Moon — means that flying is 100 easy. Our Cessna could get into the air under pedal power.

**20** In fact, humans on Titan could fly by muscle power. A human in a hang glider could comfortably take off and cruise around powered by oversized swim-flipper boots — or even take off by flapping artificial wings. The power requirements are minimal — it would probably take no more effort than 105 walking.

**21** The downside (there's always a downside) is the cold. It's 72 kelvin on Titan, which is about the temperature of liquid nitrogen. Judging from some numbers on heating requirements for light aircraft, I estimate that the cabin
110 of a Cessna on Titan would probably cool by about 2 degrees per minute.

**22** The batteries would help to keep themselves warm for a little while, but eventually the craft would run out of heat and crash. The Huygens probe, which descended with batteries nearly drained, taking fascinating pictures as it fell, succumbed to the cold after only a few hours on the surface. It had
115 enough time to send back a single photo after landing — the only one we have from the surface of a body beyond Mars.

**23** If humans put on artificial wings to fly, we might become Titanian versions of the Icarus story — our wings could freeze, fall apart, and send us tumbling to our deaths. But I've never seen the
120 Icarus story as a lesson about the limitations of humans. I see it as a lesson about the limitations of wax as an

adhesive. The cold of Titan is just an engineering problem. With the right refitting, and the right heat sources, a Cessna 172 could fly on Titan — and so could we.

---

### Notes

**2** carbon dioxide and rust　二酸化炭素と錆
**6** Mars, Venus, the four gas giant, Saturn's moon Titan, and the Sun　火星、金星、4つの巨大ガス惑星（木星、土星、天王星、海王星）、土星の衛星タイタン、太陽
**8** X-Plane　X プレイン。コンピュータ用のフライト・シミュレータ。航空写真や JAXA、NASA のデータを活用した緻密で詳細な景色や地形と、リアルなフライト・モデルを楽しめる最新鋭のフライト・シミュレータ。　hardcore aeronautics enthusiast　筋金入りの航空マニア　Who uses capslock a lot when talking about planes　飛行機について書くときに大文字ロックを多用する人（Caps Lock は役に立たないと揶揄されることが多い）
**9** config file　設定（構成）ファイル　inertia　慣性　Martian aircraft　火星の飛行機　supersonic ocean liner　超音速旅客船
**12** heat stress　熱応力。物体が温度変化による膨張や収縮を外部的な拘束によって妨げられたときに、物体内部に生じる抵抗力。
**13** oxygen mask and protective wetsuit　酸素マスクと防護用ウェットスーツ　sulfuric acid　硫酸
**14** category-5-hurricane-level winds　カテゴリー5（風速 70m/s 以上）の大型ハリケーン
**15** sea-level pressure　海面気圧　the layers of ammonia ice and water ice　凍ったアンモニアと粒状の氷の層
**17** bluish orb　青みがかった球体
**18** turbulence　乱気流
**19** surface pressure　表面圧力　pedal power　自転車の足こぎによる力
**20** swim-flipper boots　巨大水かき付きブーツ　artificial wings　人工翼
**21** 72 kelvin　72 ケルビン（− 201.15℃）　liquid nitrogen　液体窒素
**22** Huygens probe　ホイヘンス・プローブ。欧州宇宙機関 (ESA) の小型惑星探査機。土星探査機カッシーニに搭載され、土星の衛星タイタンに投下された。
**23** Icarus story　イーカロスの物語。イーカロスはギリシア神話に登場する人物。蝋で固めた翼によって自由自在に飛翔する力を得たが、太陽に接近し過ぎたことで蝋が溶けて翼がなくなり、墜落して死を迎えた。イーカロスの物語は人間の傲慢さやテクノロジーを批判する神話として知られている。

**Comprehension Check**

 **A** Read the sentences below and choose T(true) or F(false).

1. On worlds without plants, we don't have to use an electric motor because electric engines work only near green plants. **T / F**

2. If the plane were released close enough to the Mars to feel its atmosphere at all, it would be vaporized in less than a second. **T / F**

3. The Cessna's paint would start melting off in seconds, the plane's components would fail rapidly, and the plane would glide gently into the ground as it came apart under the heat stress. **T / F**

4. The weaker gravity and slightly denser atmosphere mean that we'd be able to struggle along a bit further before we gave in to either the cold or high winds and descended to the same fate as on Jupiter. **T / F**

5. Titan's atmosphere is thick but its gravity is light, giving it a surface pressure only 50 percent higher than Earth's with air four times as dense, so that it at least has some clouds to look at. **T / F**

**B** Select the best answer for each question.

1. In Paragraph 20-23, the author claims that
   (A) humans could survive on Titan because a human in a hang glider could comfortably take off and cruise around powered by oversized swim-flipper boots — or even take off by flapping artificial wings.
   (B) the Cessna's batteries would help to keep themselves warm for a little while, but eventually the craft would run out of heat and crash, judging from some numbers on heating requirements for light aircraft.
   (C) we might become Titanian versions of the Icarus story — our wings could freeze, fall apart, and send us tumbling to our deaths if humans put on artificial wings to fly on Titan.
   (D) humans could fly on Titan with the right refitting, and the right heat sources as if Icarus flew with his wax feathers without limitations.

2. The expression "be up to" in Paragraph 10 is closest in meaning to
   (A) appeal to
   (B) use to
   (C) apply to
   (D) be able to

3. The expression "The picture" in Paragraph 16 is closest in meaning to
   (A) situation
   (B) image
   (C) description
   (D) photo

4. The expression "succumbed to" in Paragraph 22 is closest in meaning to
   (A) grew up
   (B) build up
   (C) relented to
   (D) related to

## ✏️ Writing a Summary

**A** Determine the main idea of the following keywords.

1. X-plane

2. inertia

3. turbulence

4. Icarus (story)

**B** Summarize the passage in about 100 words.

_____

_____

_____

_____

_____

_____

## 😀💬 Discussion

Discuss and share your opinion on "interplanetary travel".

# UNIT 13
# HIGH THROW

高く投げる

## ⚙ Prepare to discuss and share your opinion

人間は、ものをどれくらい高く投げられるだろうか。

## ABC Vocabulary

Look up the following words and phrases in a dictionary.

| | | | | |
|---|---|---|---|---|
| accurate | projectile | evolution | millisecond | rotate |
| redirect | subtract | giraffe | plausible | altitude |

## How high can a human throw something?

—Irish Dave on the Isle of Man

ANSWER

 **Reading** ————————————————————— 🔊 Audio 2-05

**1** HUMANS ARE GOOD AT throwing things. In fact, we're great at it; no other animal can throw stuff like we can. It's true that chimpanzees hurl feces (and, on rare occasions, stones), but they're not nearly as accurate or precise as humans. Antlions throw sand, but they don't aim it. Archerfish hunt insects by throwing water droplets, but they use specialized mouths 5 instead of arms. Horned lizards shoot jets of blood from their eyes for distances of up to 5 feet. I don't know *why* they do this because whenever I reach the phrase "shoot jets of blood from their eyes" in an article I just stop there and stare at it until I need to

10 lie down.

**2** So while there are other animals that use projectiles, we're just about the only animal that can grab a random object and reliably nail a target. In fact, we're so good at it that some researchers have suggested that rock-throwing played a central role in the

15 evolution of the modern human brain.

**3** Throwing is hard [ ▷ Citation: my Little League career.]. In order to deliver a baseball to a batter, a pitcher has to release the ball at exactly the right point in the throw. A timing error of half a millisecond in either direction is enough to cause the ball to miss the strike zone.

20 **4** To put that in perspective, it takes about *five* milliseconds for the fastest nerve impulse to travel the length of the arm. That means that when your arm is still rotating toward the correct position, the signal to release the ball is already at your wrist. In terms of timing, this is like a drummer dropping a drumstick from the tenth story

25 and hitting a drum on the ground *on the correct beat.*

**5** We seem to be much better at throwing things forward than throwing them upward [ ▷ Counterexample: my Little League career]. Since we're going for maximum height, we could use projectiles that curve upward when you throw them forward; the Aerobie Orbiters I had when I was a kid often got stuck in the

30 highest treetops [ ▷ Where they remained forever.]. But we could also sidestep the whole problem by using a device like this one:

*A mechanism for hitting yourself in the head with a baseball after a four-second delay*

**6** We could use a springboard, a greased chute, or even a dangling sling — anything that redirects the object upward without adding to or subtracting from its speed. Of course,

35 we could also try this:

**7** I ran through the basic aerodynamic calculations for a baseball thrown at various speeds. I will give these heights in units of giraffes:

**8** The average person can probably throw a baseball at least three giraffes high:

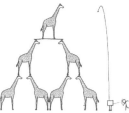

**9** Someone with a reasonably good arm could manage five:                          40

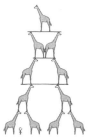

**10** A pitcher with an 80 mph fastball could manage ten giraffes:

**11** Aroldis Chapman, the holder of the world record for fastest recorded pitch (105 mph), could in theory launch a baseball 14 giraffes high:

**12** But what about projectiles other than a baseball? Obviously, with the aid of tools like slings, crossbows, or the curves *xistera* scoops in jai alai, we can launch projectiles much faster than that. But for this question, let's assume we stick to bare-handed throwing.

**13** A baseball is probably not the ideal projectile, but it's hard to find speed data on other kinds of thrown objects. Fortunately, a British javelin thrower named Roald Bradstock held a "random object throwing competition," in which he threw everything from dead fish to an actual kitchen sink. Bradstock's experience gives us a lot of useful data [ ▷ And a lot of other date, too.]. In particular, it suggests a potentially superior projectile: a golf ball.

**14** Few professional athletes have been recorded throwing golf balls. Fortunately, Bradstock has, and he claims a record throw of 170 yards. This involved a running start, but even so, it's reason to think that a golf ball might work better than a baseball. From a physics standpoint, it makes sense; the limiting factor in baseball pitches is the torque on the elbow, and the lighter golf ball might allow the pitching arm to move slightly faster.

**15** The speed improvement from using a golf ball instead of a baseball would probably not be very large, but it seems plausible that a professional pitcher with some time to practice could throw a golf ball faster than a baseball.

**16** If so, based on aerodynamic calculations, Aroldis Chapman could probably throw a golf ball about sixteen giraffes high:

**17** This is probably about the maximum possible altitude for a thrown object. ...unless you count the technique by which any five-year-old can beat all these records easily.

## Notes

**1** **antlion** アリジゴク（昆虫）　**archerfish** テッポウウオ（魚）　**water droplet** 水滴　**horned lizard** ツノトカゲ

**2** **modern human brain** 現生人類の脳

**4** **the fastest nerve impulse** 最速の神経インパルス。神経線維の中を伝わっていく活動電位。

*on the correct beat* 正確なリズムに合わせて

**5** **Aerobie Orbiters** エアロオービター。正三角形構造のブーメラン。

**6** **a springboard, a greased chute, or even a dangling sling** （体操の）踏切板、（潤滑剤の）グリースを塗った滑り台、あるいは高いところからぶら下がっているひも

**10** **80 mph** 時速80マイル（mile per hour）。130キロメートル。

**11** **Aroldis Chapman, the holder of the world record for fastest recorded pitch** 球速世界最高記録保持者のアロルディス・チャップマン。キューバ共和国出身のプロ野球選手。MLB史上最速となる105.1 mph（169.1 km/h）の記録を保持し、ギネス世界記録にも認定された。

**12** **slings** 投石器。石を遠くへ投げるためのひも状の道具（武器）。　**crossbows** クロスボウ。専用の矢を板ばねの力で弦により発射する弓（武器）。　*xistera* システラ。ハイアライで使われる道具。　**jai alai** ハイアライ。ヨーロッパのバスク地方（フランス・スペイン）発祥の球技。セスタと呼ばれるグローブを右手に装着し、遠心力でボールを加速させてから、壁に向かってボールを投げつける競技。

**13** **Roald Bradstock** ロアルド・ブラッドストック。イギリスの槍投げ選手。　**random object throwing competition** 手当たり次第にものを投げる競争

**14** **170 yards** 170ヤード（約155.4メートル）　**limiting factor** 制約となる因子。ある事象や現象、働きが複数の要素の影響で起こる場合に、その全体の働き方を決める要素のこと。　**torque** トルク。軸などの棒状の物体をねじる方向の力。ねじりモーメント。回転力。

 ## Comprehension Check

**A** Read the sentences below and choose T(true) or F(false).

1. Although there are other animals that use projectiles, we're just about the only animal that can grab a random object and reliably nail a target.　**T / F**

2. It takes about five milliseconds for the fastest nerve impulse to travel the length of the arm, which means that this is like a drummer dropping a drumstick from the tenth story of a building.　**T / F**

3. The average person can probably throw a baseball at least three giraffes high, while someone with a reasonably good arm could manage five.　**T / F**

4. Even though Bradstock claims a record throw of 170 yards, few professional athletes have been recorded throwing golf balls.　**T / F**

5. From a physics standpoint, the limiting factor in baseball pitches is the moment of force on the elbow, and the lighter golf ball might allow the pitching arm to move slightly faster.　**T / F**

**B** Select the best answer for each question.

1. In Paragraph 12-17, the author claims that
   (A) we should launch projectiles much faster than golf ball with the aid of tools like slings, crossbows, or the curves *xistera* scoops in jai alai.
   (B) the holder of the world record involved a running start, but even so, it's reason to think that a golf ball might work better than a dead fish and an actual kitchen sink.
   (C) the speed improvement from using a golf ball would probably be very large, so it seems credible that a professional pitcher with some time to practice could throw a golf ball faster than a baseball.
   (D) about sixteen giraffes high is probably about the maximum possible altitude for a thrown object unless you count the technique by which any five-year-old can beat all these records easily.

2. The expression "on rare occasions" in Paragraph 1 is closest in meaning to
   (A) typically
   (B) generally
   (C) frequently
   (D) rarely

3. The word "story" in Paragraph 4 is closest in meaning to
   (A) narrative
   (B) floor
   (C) room
   (D) description

4. The expression "stick to" in Paragraph 12 is closest in meaning to
   (A) fail to
   (B) associate with
   (C) cling to
   (D) deal out

 Writing a Summary

 Determine the main idea of the following keywords.

1. nerve impulse

2. jai alai

3.  limiting factor

4.  torque

**B** Summarize the passage in about 100 words.

_____

_____

_____

_____

_____

_____

## Discussion

Discuss and share your opinion on "how to raise the balloon".

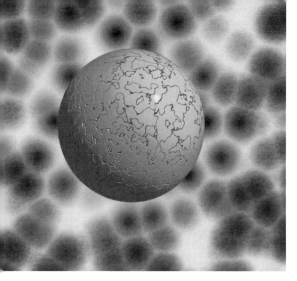

# UNIT 14
# LETHAL
# NEUTRINOS
死に至るニュートリノ

 **Prepare to discuss and share your opinion**

どのくらい超新星に接近したら、致死量のニュートリノを浴びることになるだろうか。

 **Vocabulary**

Look up the following words and phrases in a dictionary.

| | | | | |
|---|---|---|---|---|
| lethal | dose | radiation | incongruous | background |
| retina | detonation | unimaginable | insubstantial | reinforce |

How close would you have to be to a supernova to get a lethal dose of neutrino radiation?

—Dr. Donald Spector

(ANSWER)

**Reading** ━━━━━━━━━━━━━━━━━━━━━━━━━━━━━ 🔊 Audio 2-06

**1** THE PHRASE "LETHAL DOSE of neutrino radiation" is a weird one. I had to turn it over in my head a few times after I heard it. If you're not a physics person, it might not sound odd to you, so here's a little context why it's such a surprising idea:

5 **2** Neutrinos are ghostly particles that barely interact with the world at all. Look at your hand — there are about a trillion neutrinos from the Sun passing through it every second.

*Okay, you can stop looking at your hand now.*

**3** The reason you don't notice the neutrino flood is that neutrinos mostly ignore ordinary matter. On average, out of that massive flood, only one neutrino will "hit" an atom in your body every few years [ ▷ Less often if you're a child, since you have fewer atoms to be hit. Statistically, your first neutrino interaction probably happens somewhere around age ten.].

**4** In fact, neutrinos are so shadowy that the entire Earth is transparent to them; nearly all of the Sun's neutrino steam goes straight through it unaffected. To detect neutrinos, people build giant tanks filled with hundreds of tons of target material in the hopes that they'll register the impact of a single solar neutrino.

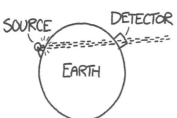

**5** This means that when a particle accelerator (which produces neutrinos) wants to send a neutrino beam to a detector somewhere else in the world, all it has to do is point the beam at the detector — even if it's on the other side of the Earth!

**6** That's why the phrase "lethal dose of neutrino radiation" sounds weird — it mixes scales in an incongruous way. It's like the idiom "knock me over with a feather" or the phrase "football stadium filled to the brim with ants." [ ▷ Which would still be less than 1 percent of the ants in the world.] If you have a math background, it's sort of like seeing the expression "$\ln(x)^e$" — it's not that, taken literally, it doesn't make sense — it's that you can't imagine a situation where it would apply [ ▷ If you want to be mean to first-year calculus students, you can ask them to take the derivative of $\ln(x)^e dx$. It looks like it should be "1" or something, but it's not.].

**7** Similarly, it's hard to produce enough neutrinos to get even a single *one* of them to interact with matter; it's strange to imagine a scenario in which there'd be enough of them to hurt you.

**8** Supernovae provide that scenario [ ▷ "Supernovas" is also fine. "Supernovii" is discouraged.]. Dr. Spector, the Hobart and William Smith Colleges physicist who asked me this question, told me his rule of thumb for estimating supernova-related numbers: However big you think supernovae are, they're bigger than that.

**9** Here's a question to give you a sense of scale. Which of the following
would be brighter, in terms of the amount of energy delivered to your retina:
**10** A supernova, seen from as far away as the Sun is from the Earth, or the
detonation of a hydrogen bomb *pressed against your eyeball?*

*Can you hurry up and set it off? This is heavy.*

**11** Applying Dr. Spector's rule of thumb suggests that the supernova is
brighter. And indeed, it is... by *nine orders of magnitude.*

**12** That's why this is a neat question — supernovae are unimaginably huge
and neutrinos are unimaginably insubstantial. At what point do these two
unimaginable things cancel out to produce an effect on a human scale?

**13** A paper by radiation expert Andrew Karam provides an answer. It
explains that during certain supernovae, the collapse of a stellar core into a
neutron star, $10^{57}$ neutrinos can be released (one for every proton in the star
that collapses to become a neutron).

**14** Karam calculates that the neutrino radiation dose at a distance of 1
parsec [ ▷ 3.262 light-years, or a little less than the distance from here to Alpha Centauri.] would be
around half a nanosievert, or 1/500th the dose from eating a banana [ ▷ "Radiation
Dose Chart," http://xkcd.com/radiation.].

**15** A fatal radiation dose is about 4 sieverts. Using the inverse-square law,
we can calculate the radiation dose:

$$0.5 \text{ nanosieverts} \times \left(\tfrac{1 \text{ parsec}}{x}\right)^2 = 5 \text{ sieverts}$$
$$x = 0.00001118 \text{ parsecs} = 2.3 \text{ AU}$$

**16** That's a little more than the distance between the Sun and Mars. Core-
collapse supernovae happen to giant stars, so if you observed a supernova
from that distance, you'd probably be inside the outer layers of the star that

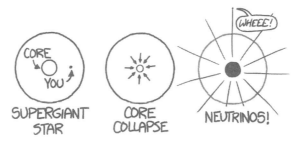

*GRB 080319B was the most violent event ever observed—*
*especially for the people who were floating right next to it with surfboards.*

created it.

**17** The idea of neutrino radiation damage reinforces just how big supernovae are. If you observed a supernova from 1 AU away — and you somehow avoided being incinerated, vaporized, and converted to some type of exotic plasma — even the flood of ghostly neutrinos would be dense enough to kill you. If it's going fast enough, a feather can *absolutely* knock you over. 65

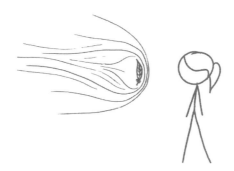

---
**Notes** ─────────────

**2** neutrino  ニュートリノ。素粒子のうちの中性レプトンの名称。

**4** To detect neutrinos, people build giant tanks...  スーパーカミオカンデ（ニュートリノを観測するために、岐阜県に設置された観測装置）のことに言及していると思われる。　solar neutrino  太陽ニュートリノ。核融合の結果、太陽で生成される電子ニュートリノ。

**5** particle accelerator （ニュートリノを作り出す）粒子加速器

**6** calculus  微積分学　derivative  導関数

**8** supernovae  超新星（supernova の複数形）。大質量の恒星が、その一生を終えるときに起こす大規模な爆発現象のこと。Hobart and William Smith Colleges  ホバート・アンド・ウィリアム・スミス・カレッジ。ニューヨーク州ジュネーブにある私立リベラル・アーツ・カレッジ。　supernova-related numbers  超新星に関連する数量

**10** hydrogen bomb  水素爆弾

**11** *nine orders of magnitude*  9 桁分

**13** neutron star  中性子星。質量の大きな恒星が進化した最晩年の天体の一種。　proton  陽子

**14** parsec  パーセク。主として天文学で使われる天体の距離を表す計量単位。　Alpha Centauri  アルファ・ケンタウリ星。ケンタウルス座で最も明るい星であり、銀河系の恒星のうち最も太陽に近い恒星である。　Radiation Dose Chart  線量表

**15** fatal radiation dose  致命的な放射線量　sievert  シーベルト。生体の被曝による生物学的影響の大きさを表す単位。　inverse-square law  逆 2 乗の法則。物理量がその発生源からの距離の 2 乗に反比例するという法則。　AU=Astronomical Unit  太陽系内の天体間の距離を測定するための天文学で用いられる距離の単位。1AU ＝ 149597870km。

**16** core-collapse supernovae  中心核が崩壊した超新星　outer layers of the star  恒星の外層

**17** neutrino radiation damage  ニュートリノ放射によるダメージ

## Comprehension Check

 **A** Read the sentences below and choose T(true) or F(false).

1. Although there are about a trillion neutrinos from the Sun passing through it every second, the reason you don't notice the neutrino flood is that neutrinos mostly ignore ordinary mater. **T / F**

2. The whole earth is transparent to neutrinos because neutrinos are almost unsubstantial; nearly all of the Sun's neutrino steam goes straight through it unaffected. **T / F**

3. It's hard to produce enough neutrinos to get even a single one of them to interact with matter as Dr. Spector told me his rule of thumb for estimating supernova-related numbers. **T / F**

4. Supernovae are unimaginably huge and neutrinos are unimaginable insubstantial; these two unimaginable things cancel out to produce an effect on a human scale. **T / F**

5. Andrew Karam insists that the neutrino radiation dose at a distance of 1 parsec would be around half a nanosievert, or 1/500th the dose from eating a banana. **T / F**

**B** Select the best answer for each question.

1. In Paragraph 1-17, the author claims that
   (A) people build giant tanks filled with hundreds of tons of target material in the hopes that they'll register the impact of a single solar neutrino to generate neutrinos.
   (B) a particle accelerator which produces neutrinos enables us to send a neutrino beam to the other side of the Earth.
   (C) while core-collapse supernovae would be probably inside the outer layers of the star that created it, the idea of neutrino radiation damage reinforces just how big supernovae are.
   (D) the flood of ghostly neutrinos would be concentrated in a very dense enough to kill you if you observed a supernova from 1AU away and you somehow avoided being extinguished.

2. The idiom "knock me over with a feather" in Paragraph 6 is closest in meaning to
   (A) knock on
   (B) surprised
   (C) threatened
   (D) felled

3. The expression "rule of thumb" in Paragraph 8 is closest in meaning to
   (A) trial and error
   (B) experimental rule
   (C) unwritten rule
   (D) hit and miss

4. The expression "cancel out" in Paragraph 12 is closest in meaning to
   (A) revoke
   (B) prohibit
   (C) abolish
   (D) counterbalance

## ✎ Writing a Summary

**A** Determine the main idea of the following keywords.

1. neutrino


2. particle accelerator


3. supernova


4. Alpha Centauri


**B** Summarize the passage in about 100 words.

_____

_____

_____

_____

_____

_____

## 😊 Discussion

Discuss and share your opinion on "a fatal radiation dose".

# UNIT 15
# SPEED BUMP

スピードバンプ

 **Prepare to discuss and share your opinion**

車でスピードバンプ（自動車を減速させるために作られた隆起）に乗り上げても死に至らない速度はどのくらいだろうか。

 **Vocabulary**

Look up the following words and phrases in a dictionary.

| | | | | |
|---|---|---|---|---|
| disclaimer | sizable | proportionally | absorb | permanently |
| compress | substantial | airfoil | disassemble | reenter |

## How fast can you hit a speed bump while driving and live?

—Myrlin Barber

ANSWER

 **Reading** ·························································· 📶 Audio 2-07

**1** SURPRISINGLY FAST. First, a disclaimer. After reading this answer, don't try to drive over speed bumps at high speeds. Here are some reasons:

· You could hit and kill someone.

5 · It can destroy your tires, suspension, and potentially your entire car.

· Have you *read* any of the other answers in this book?

**2** If that's not enough, here are some quotes from medical journals on spinal injury from speed bumps.

> *Examination of the thoracolumbar X-ray and computed tomography displayed* 10
> *compression fractures in four patients…Posterior instrumentation was*
> *applied…All patients recovered well except for the one with cervical fracture.*

> *L1 was the most frequently fractured vertebra (23/52,44.2 percent).*

> *Incorporation of the buttocks with realistic properties diminished the first*
> *vertical natural frequency from ~12 to 5.5 Hz, in agreement with the literature.* 15

(The last one isn't directly related to speed bump injuries but I wanted to include it anyway.)

## Regular little speed bumps probably won't kill you

**3** Speed bumps are designed to make drivers slow down. Going over a typical speed bump at 5 miles per hour results in a gentle bounce,[1] while 20 hitting one at 20 delivers a sizable jolt. It's natural to assume that hitting a speed bump at 60 would deliver a proportionally larger jolt, but it probably wouldn't.

**4** As those medical quotes attest, it's true that people are occasionally injured by speed bumps. However, nearly all of those injuries happen to a 25 very specific category of people: those sitting in hard seats in the backs of buses, riding on poorly maintained roads.

**5** When you're driving a car, the two main things protecting you from bumps in the road are the tires and the suspension. No matter how fast you hit a speed bump, unless the bump is large enough to hit the frame of 30 the car, enough of the jolt will be absorbed by these two systems that you probably won't be hurt.

**6** Absorbing the shock won't necessarily be *good* for those systems. In the case of the tires, they may absorb it by exploding [ ▷ Just Google "hit a curb at 60."]. If the bump is large enough to hit the wheel rims, it may permanently damage 35 a lot of important parts of the car.

**7** The typical speed bump is between 3 and 4 inches tall. That's also about how thick an average tire's cushion is (the separation between the bottom of the rims and the ground) [ ▷ There are cars everywhere. Go outside with a ruler and check.]. This means that if a car hits a small speed bump, the rim won't actually touch the 40 bump; the tire will just be compressed.

**8** The typical sedan has a top speed of around 120 miles per hour. Hitting a speed bump at that speed would, in one way or another, probably result in losing control of the car and crashing [ ▷ At high speeds, you can easily lose control even without hitting a bump. Joey Huneycutt's 220-mph crash left his Camaro a burned-out hulk.]. However, the jolt *itself* probably wouldn't be fatal.

**9** If you hit a larger speed bump — like a speed hump or speed table — your car might not fare so well.

### How fast would you have to go to definitely die?

**10** Let's consider what would happen if a car were going *faster* than its top speed. The average modern car is limited to a top speed of around 120 mph, and the fastest can go about 200.

**11** While most passenger cars have some kind of artificial speed limits imposed by the engine computer, the ultimate physical limit to a car's top speed comes from air resistance. This type of drag increases with the square of speed; at some point, a car doesn't have enough engine power to push through the air any faster.

**12** If you *did* force a sedan to go faster than its top speed — perhaps by reusing the magical accelerator from the relativistic baseball — the speed bump would be the least of your problems. Cars generate lift. The air flowing around a car exerts all kinds of forces on it.

*Where did all these arrows come from?*

**13** The lift forces are relatively minor at normal highway speeds, but at higher speeds, they become substantial. In a Formula One car equipped with airfoils, this force pushes downward, holding the car against the track. In a sedan, they lift it up.

**14** Among NASCAR fans, there's frequently talk of a 200-mph "liftoff speed" if the car starts to spin. Other branches of auto racing have seen spectacular backflip crashes when the aerodynamics don't work out as planned. The bottom line is that in the range of 150-300 mph, a typical sedan would lift off the ground, tumble, and crash...before you even hit the bump.  70

*BREAKING: Child, Unidentified Creature in Bicycle Basket Hit and Killed by Car*

**15** If you kept the car from taking off, the force of the wind at those speeds would strip away the hood, side panels, and windows. At higher speeds, the car itself would be disassembled, and might even burn up like a spacecraft reentering the atmosphere.

**What's the ultimate limit?**  75

**16** In the state of Pennsylvania, drivers may see $2 added to their speeding ticket for every mile per hour by which they break the speed limit. Therefore, if you drove a car over a Philadelphia speed bump at 90 percent of the speed of light, in addition to destroying the city...

**17** ...you could expect a speeding ticket of $1.14 billion.  80

**┌─ Notes ───────────────────────────────────────┐**

**②medical journal** 医学誌 **spinal injury** 脊髄損傷
***Examination of the thoracolumbar X-ray and computed tomography*** 胸腰部 X 線撮影およびコンピュータ
トモグラフィーによる検査 **compression fracture** 圧迫骨折 **posterior instrumentation** 脊椎インストゥルメン
テーション。(金具などを挿入して固定する手術)。 **cervical fracture** 頸椎骨折 **L1** 第一腰椎 **vertebra** 椎骨 **first
vertical natural frequency** 第一垂直自然周波数
**⑧sedan** セダン。車体形状や使用形態により分類される自動車の形態の 1 つ。 **Camaro** シボレー・カマロ。アメリカの
スポーツカー。 **a burned-out hulk** 焼け焦げた残骸
**⑨speed hump** スピードハンプ。スピードバンプを大型化したもの。 **speed table** スピードテーブル。通常のスピー
ドハンプより長くしたもの。
**⑪air resistance** 空気抵抗
**⑫the magical accelerator from the relativistic baseball** 相対論的野球のときに使った魔法の加速器。UNIT1 を参照。
**⑬lift force** 揚力。上向きに働く力、浮揚力。 **Formula One car** F1 カー
**⑭NASCAR fan** 全米自動車競走協会 (National Association for Stock Car Auto Racing) 主催の自動車レースのファン
**liftoff speed** 離陸速度 **spectacular backflip crash** 劇的な後方宙返り **Unidentified Creature** 地球外生物。子
どもの自転車のカゴの中にいる地球外生物とは、映画 *E.T.* (1982) を連想させる。
**⑯the state of Pennsylvania** ペンシルベニア州 **speeding ticket** スピード違反の切符 **Philadelphia** フィラデル
フィア。アメリカ合衆国ペンシルベニア州南東部にある都市。

**└────────────────────────────────────────────┘**

 ## Comprehension Check ─────────────────────────────

 **A** Read the sentences below and choose T(true) or F(false).

1. Going over a typical speed bump at 5 miles per hour contributes to a gentle bounce, while hitting one at 20 delivers a sizable jolt. **T / F**

2. Hitting a speed bump at around 120 miles per hour would probably result in losing control of the car and crashing though the jolt itself probably wouldn't be fatal.

   **T / F**

3. Most cars have some kind of artificial speed limit imposed by the engine computer, but the ultimate physical limit to the car's maximum speed comes from air resistance. **T / F**

4. The lift forces are relatively substantial at normal highway speeds so that the air flowing around a car exerts all kinds of forces on it and generates lift. **T / F**

5. Even if you kept the car from taking off, the force of the wind at those speeds would rip off the hood, side panels, and windows. **T / F**

**B**  Select the best answer for each question.

1.  In Paragraph 1-17, the author claims that
    (A) it's true that the people who sitting in hard seats in the backs of buses are inevitably injured by speed bumps.
    (B) you probably will be hurt by virtues of tires and suspension unless absorbing the shock is not necessarily be good for those systems.
    (C) a car doesn't have enough engine power to push through the air any faster because the air flowing around a car exerts all kinds of forces on it.
    (D) drivers could see $2 added to their speeding ticket by which they broke the speed limit if you drove a car over a Philadelphia speed bump at 90 percent of the speed of light.

2.  The word "the literature" in Paragraph 2 is closest in meaning to
    (A) the documents
    (B) the novel
    (C) the poetry
    (D) the information

3.  The word "gentle" in Paragraph 3 is closest in meaning to
    (A) affable
    (B) quiet
    (C) peaceful
    (D) harsh

4.  The word "substantial" in Paragraph 13 is closest in meaning to
    (A) actual
    (B) heavy
    (C) significant
    (D) solid

 Writing a Summary

**A**  Determine the main idea of the following keywords.

1.  speed bump

2.  air resistance

**3.** liftoff speed

**4.** speeding ticket

**B** Summarize the passage in about 100 words.

_____

_____

_____

_____

_____

_____

 **Discussion**

Discuss and share your opinion on "the ultimate limit".

# RANDALL MUNROE'S NOTES

## UNIT 1

1. After I initially published this article, MIT physicist Hans Rinderknecht contacted me to say that he'd simulated this scenario on their lab's computers. He found that early in the ball's flight, most of the air molecules were actually moving too quickly to cause fusion, and would pass right through the ball, heating it more slowly and uniformly than my original article described.

## UNIT 5

1. That's a neat coincidence I've never noticed before—a cubic mile happens to be almost exactly $4/3\pi$ cubic kilometers, so a sphere with a radius of X kilometers has the same volume as a cube that's X miles on each side.

## UNIT 6

1. Judging by the amount of ammunition they had lying around their house ready to measure and weigh for me, Texas has apparently become some kind of Mad-Max-esque post-apocalyptic war zone.

   ▶ Mad-Max-esque post-apocalyptic war zone 映画『マッドマックス』風の世界滅亡後の戦争地帯

## UNIT 8

1. This is why, even though matches and torches are about the same temperature, you see tough guys in movies extinguish matches by pinching them but never see them do the same with torches.

## UNIT 9

1. Although not everyone sees it this way. Mallory Ortberg, writing on the-toast. net, characterized the story of The Little Prince as a wealthy child demanding that a plane crash survivor draw him pictures, then critiquing his drawing style.
2. …which is why it should really be called "escape speed" — the fact that it has no direction (which is the distinction between "speed" and "velocity") is unexpectedly significant here.

## UNIT 10

1. The residents of St. Kilda correctly identified the boats as the trigger for the outbreaks. The medical experts of the time, however, dismissed these claims, instead blaming the outbreaks on the way the islanders stood around outdoors in the cold when a boat arrived, and on their celebrating the new arrivals by drinking too much.

## UNIT 15

1. Like anyone with a physics background, I do all my calculations in SI units, but I've gotten too many US speeding tickets to write this answer in anything but miles per hour; it's just been burned into my brain. Sorry!

▶ **SI unit** 国際単位系。metre, kilogram, second, ampere, kelvin, candela, mole の七つがある。

*What If?: Serious Scientific Answers to Absurd Hypothetical Questions* by Randall Munroe © xkcd Inc. 2014

Reproduced by permission of John Murray Press, an imprint of Hodder and Stoughton Limited.

---

**What If?:** Serious Scientific Answers to Absurd Hypothetical Questions
科学の答え：地球上の全人類がジャンプして同時に地面に降りたらどうなるか

---

2020 年 4 月 10 日　初版第 1 刷発行

編著者　小林亜希

発行者　森　信久
発行所　**株式会社　松柏社**
〒 102-0072　東京都千代田区飯田橋 1-6-1
TEL　03 (3230) 4813（代表）
FAX　03 (3230) 4857
http://www.shohakusha.com
e-mail: info@shohakusha.com

英文校閲　　Howard Colefield
装　　幀　　小島トシノブ（NONdesign）
印刷・製本　日経印刷株式会社

ISBN978-4-88198-756-8

略号＝ 756